The True Cost
of Low Prices

The True Cost of Low Prices

The Violence of Globalization

Vincent A. Gallagher

ORBIS BOOKS

Maryknoll, New York 10545

Founded in 1970, Orbis Books endeavors to publish works that enlighten the mind, nourish the spirit, and challenge the conscience. The publishing arm of the Maryknoll Fathers and Brothers, Orbis seeks to explore the global dimensions of the Christian faith and mission, to invite dialogue with diverse cultures and religious traditions, and to serve the cause of reconciliation and peace. The books published reflect the views of their authors and do not represent the official position of the Maryknoll Society. To learn more about Maryknoll and Orbis Books, please visit our website at www.maryknoll.org.

Library of Congress Cataloging-in-Publication Data

Gallagher, Vincent A.
    The true cost of low prices : the violence of globalization / Vincent A. Gallagher.
        p.   cm.
    Includes bibliographical references and index.
    ISBN-13: 978-1-57075-669-6 (pbk.)
    1. International trade – Social aspects. 2. Poverty – Developing countries. 3. Labor – Social aspects – Developing countries.   I. Title.
HF1413.G25 2006
306.3 – dc22
                                                                    2006009992

Contents

Acknowledgments

I am most appreciative to all the people who serve at the Romero Center at St. Joseph Pro-Cathedral Parish in Camden, New Jersey. The Romero Center serves as a bridge between culture and gospel by bringing high school and college students and others in touch with the people of Camden, one of the poorest, most violent cities in the United States. After making dozens of presentations to groups at the Romero Center about the themes of this book, I decided to put it all together. So thanks to Father Bob McDermott, Pat Slater, Larry DePaul, Teresa Reyes, Frederick Pratt, April Gagne, Brian Reese, Barbara Thomas, Sarah Flounders, and Kevin Moran. If I had not had the opportunity to serve at the Romero Center, I would never have thought of this book. The people who serve at the Romero Center are surely instruments of God's love.

Thanks especially for the helpful suggestions of my editor, Susan Perry, whose kind and thoughtful guidance taught me well. And thanks also for the suggestions and guidance of Marie Dennis of the Maryknoll Office for Global Concerns, Dale Stitt of Journey into Freedom, Megan and Brian Gallagher, Maureen Gallagher-Boland, Marty Owens, and Ron Bean. Some very good friends whom I met in Lima, Peru, were also a great inspiration to me because of their courage, love, and humility: Immaculate Heart of Mary sisters Rosemary DePaul and Sonya Avi and Columban fathers Bob O'Rourke and John Buckley. I am grateful for all the support along the way offered by the Peacemakers of Pax Christi Southwest New Jersey: Donna and Fred

Maccherone, Denise and Bill Mattia, Colleen and John Connell, Letitia Oppecker, Mary Laubenthal, Marie Cameron, Pat and Jay VanDeevort, and Mary Rachel Austin. And a special thanks to Sister Clare Annice, S.S.J., who has been an example to me of great service and love since I was a young boy. And where would I be without the love and support of Clare McCarthy and Dick Gallagher? A special thanks to P. J. Gallagher for his photography and support in Guatemala, and to Bob O'Brien, my friend, with whom I have pondered issues of justice for decades. Thanks also to two special loving spirits, Mark Chmiel and Mev Puleo, and for Mark's permission to use Mev's photos.

A very special thanks to Katherine Farley Horcher, who has guided me in spiritual direction for many years. It is a blessing to have such a wise and kind companion. And to all of her Remnants who have inspired and supported me for many years: Keith Roland, Ernie Gunn, Jim Griffith, Frank Hollick, and Charles Carr. I greatly appreciate the help of Father John McNamee, pastor of St. Malachy's Parish in Philadelphia and author of *Diary of a City Priest*. His inspiration and help were truly instrumental. Likewise, all the work and support of Michele Szachewicz was essential. Without her help, the book simply would not exist.

I am deeply indebted to my wife, Cathy, who has supported me for many years in so many ways, especially by giving me the freedom to go off to faraway places while she tended to all the work at home. I greatly appreciate her love and support, more than I can say. I am grateful to all of the Immaculate Heart of Mary sisters and Christian Brothers and teachers from LaSalle University, especially Dr. John Grady, who taught me that the study of economics examines questions of justice. Thanks to Linda Panetta for permission to use her poem "Our Mother . . . Our Sister."

I like to think the real source of the book was the Holy Spirit. Many times through contact with abandoned children living on the streets of Latin America, with children working in the garbage dumps, with men, women, and children living and dying with AIDS and other diseases, and with other precious, lonely souls, I have had my heart broken — wide open. It was then that the Holy Spirit entered and inspired me to share what was given.

Abbreviations

AID	Agency for International Development
AIFLD	American Institute for Free Labor Development
CAFTA	Central American Free Trade Agreement
CSO	civil society organization
FGM	female genital mutilation
FTAA	Free Trade Agreement of the Americas
GATT	General Agreement on Tariffs and Trades
GNI	Gross National Income
HIPC	heavily indebted poor country
HPI	human poverty index
IMF	International Monetary Fund
LDC	less developed country
NAFTA	North American Free Trade Agreement
OSHA	Occupational Safety and Health Act
PRSP	Poverty Reduction Strategy Paper
PSI	policy support instrument
SAP	structural adjustment program
SOA	School of the Americas
UCA	University of Central America
UNDP	United Nations Development Program
UNIFEM	United Nations Development Fund for Women
USIA	United States Information Agency
WB	World Bank
WTO	World Trade Organization

Introduction

There have been massive demonstrations against globalization in Miami, Washington, Seattle, Canada, Mexico, Brazil, Argentina, Venezuela, France, Germany, Italy, England, India, the Philippines, New Zealand, Australia, Kenya, South Africa, Thailand, Malaysia, and Indonesia. Yet most Americans do not understand what the environmentalists, farmers, students, human rights activists, labor activists, religious people, and others are upset about. The Live 8 concert on July 2, 2005, helped awaken young people to the problem of the debt burden of poor countries. But few people in the developed countries understand the magnitude and severity of the injustice and injury that result from the policies of the international financial institutions that hold tremendous power over the economies of poor countries. Many people in poor countries who suffer the injustices of globalization have a much greater understanding of how it works than do most educated people in the United States. It is not easy for us to understand. The media, owned by the powerful who benefit from these arrangements, have no incentive to educate us.

It took me a long time to catch on to the notion of institutionalized violence. After graduating from college, I served in the Peace Corps in Venezuela (1964–66). There I lived among people who were poor, but I had no understanding of the connection between their suffering and the larger political reality. I just did not know how countries are connected and affected by political, legal, and economic structures. I have spent thirty-four years working in the field of worker injury and disease prevention.

1

My work has taken me into over fifteen hundred workplaces in the United States and eight countries in Latin America. I have evaluated safety and health hazards in steel mills, petrochemical and chemical companies, auto assembly plants, metal and wood product manufacturing plants, food processing facilities, electrical power generation plants, and so on. I have seen up close how workers fare when they interact with capital. The process of making things and growing and gathering food can injure, sicken, and kill. I never thought of those processes as violent until in 1980 I read a book by Camilo Torres, a Colombian priest who joined the revolutionary National Liberation Army. He pointed out that it is a violence for government and industrialists to provide health care to some and to deny others. Children die for lack of antibiotics because of political decisions. He characterized that as institutionalized violence. He saw that there was a war taking place — a silent war with casualties suffered behind closed doors.

In my professional work, I had investigated hundreds of cases of worker injury and death. I came to realize that most were caused by decisions to risk workers' lives for economic gain. For example:

- Workers lose fingers and hands when protective shields are taken off machines to increase productivity.

- Buildings can be constructed more quickly if fall protection is not implemented. Sometimes workers fall and can suffer paraplegia, quadriplegia, brain damage, or death. It takes time and costs money to work safely in compliance with safety laws.

- Food processing equipment can be cleaned more quickly if it is not shut down and the power locked out. Rather, if it is kept running, the protective guards are taken off, and then it is sprayed and cleaned, the job will be done much more quickly. But workers may lose hands, arms, or feet.

* Hundreds of thousands of workers have suffered asbestosis and death from lung disease and five types of cancer caused by exposure to asbestos because ventilation systems were not installed and workers were required to follow unsafe practices that violate safety laws.

The list of examples of the ways workers suffer injury, disease, and death because factory owners try to save money by not controlling hazards could go on and on.

We think of violence as a sudden act that results in injury. But violence occurs from business and government decisions that are just as cruel as the use of a machete or a gun. The difference is just a matter of time.

It is violent to cut someone's hand off with a machete. But isn't it also violent to produce goods with unguarded machines that amputate as surely and brutally as machetes?

Isn't it violent if an entire *campesino* (farm worker) community suffers central nervous system disorders, brain damage, birth defects, nightmares, suicides, or death from exposure to highly toxic pesticides banned in the developed countries but marketed by transnational corporations throughout the poor nations?

Isn't it violent when people get sick and die from drinking water polluted by a multinational corporation that invested in that country precisely because of a lack of environmental and worker rights laws?

It is violent to cut out a person's heart or lung. But isn't it violent to manufacture toxic products without controlling the gases, vapors, dust, fumes, and fibers that cause lung disease, heart disease, cancer and birth defects?

Isn't it violent to use unsafe mining methods that increase production but cause lung disease, slow suffocation, and premature death among miners?

It is violent to snuff out the life of a child. But isn't it violent when the International Monetary Fund requires the Ministry of Health in a poor country to cut funding so that government hospitals have no antibiotics or other drugs to prevent the death of children?

It is violent to choke children. But isn't it violent for companies in developed countries to sell poor countries recalled dangerous toys with parts that can be swallowed and so causing children to die of choking?

If your child works at the dump recycling paper, bottles, plastic, and cans and is exposed to the hazards of biological, industrial, and human waste because your ability to buy food is limited by the devaluation of your currency imposed by the International Monetary Fund, would you see that as a form of violence?

There is enough food to feed everybody, yet more than 800 million people in poor countries suffer from malnutrition.[1] It is estimated that thirty-five thousand children die every day from diseases related to malnutrition.[2] Isn't that a form of violence?

On occasion, we see images of a mother holding a starving child. But we don't realize that this injustice results primarily from political and economic structures that essentially institutionalize injustice. For example, we don't see:

- how the structural adjustment policies imposed on poor countries by the international lenders force poor children to leave school to live and work on the streets, in the garbage dumps, in factories, or in the sex trade.

- how government troops murdering activist priests and raping and killing nuns in El Salvador is related to the low prices we pay for sugar, coffee, cocoa, and cotton.

- how sexual abuse and harassment of young women in the clothing industries in the Third World is related to the price of our clothes.

Boy living on the street in Bogotá, Colombia.

* how asbestos, banned in developed countries but sold by multi-national corporations in Latin America, is causing asbestosis and cancer among millions of workers and the public in Latin America.

* how our investments in retirement plans and mutual funds support companies that exploit the most desperate workers and supply arms and tobacco that wreak havoc on the poor.

Euro-American history shows that education and hard work results in each generation getting more. The grandchildren of European immigrants go to college and move from the inner city to suburbs. Their children go to graduate school, law school, medical schools. Many middle-class children live in communities where no one they know experiences hunger or a lack of clothing, shelter, or health care.

We don't see a link between the wealth of our nation and the genocide of indigenous people, colonialism, slavery, exploitation of immigrant labor, and the continuing brutal exploitation of labor by way of a neocolonial system that dominates and draws the life out of the poor.

◆ ◆ ◆

The progression in this book is from head to heart — the longest of journeys. First it considers how the political, economic, legal, and military structures are organized or institutionalized to exploit the poor. It then considers the effects of this injustice. It describes the uses of women, children, and slaves in the global economy. Finally it reflects on the theology of liberation and what it means for rich Christians. It is not enough to understand. The reign of God of which Jesus spoke so often comes about, not from understanding, but from love.

One of the last books that Tolstoy wrote was entitled *The Kingdom of God Is within You.* It was just before the Russian Revolution. He was on a train with soldiers and officers who were going to forcefully evict squatters who were accused of living on a rich man's land. Tolstoy said everyone knew the judge who gave the eviction order was corrupted by the wealthy. The soldiers were going to slaughter the peasants.

Tolstoy said that the soldiers and officers were very nice people. They played cards and drank beer. The officers wrote to their families, and no one talked about what was about to happen. He said no one person can stop the wave of the forces of history that pour over us. But the most important first thing to do, which can be done, is to at least tell the truth.

We need to wake each other up. Many of us have no awareness of the brutality of the economic and political structures that suck the life of the poor. Many of us practice a narrow theology far from true gospel values. Many of us are blinded by our self-righteousness.

IN PRAISE OF SELF-DEPRECATION

The buzzard has nothing to fault himself with.
Scruples are alien to the black panther.
Piranhas do not doubt the rightness of their actions.
The rattlesnake approves of himself without reservations.

The self-critical jackal does not exist.
The locust, alligator, trichina, horsefly
live as they live and are glad of it.

The killer-whale's heart weighs one hundred kilos
but in other respects it is light.

There is nothing more animal-like
than a clear conscience
on the third planet of the Sun.[3]

—Wislawa Szymborska from *Sounds, Feelings, Thoughts,*
trans. Magnus J. Krynski, © Princeton University Press.
Reprinted by permission of Princeton University Press.

Many of us have a clear conscience about the United States having accumulated and possessing more wealth than any other country. Few understand how our lifestyles are supported by the blood, sweat, and tears of very poor people, most of whom are women, and some of whom are children or slaves.

Hasidic rabbi Levi Yitzhak of the Ukraine tells this story. The rabbi visited the owner of a tavern. Two peasants were at a table. They were drinking with reckless abandon with arms around each other saying how much they loved each other. Ivan said to Peter: "Peter, tell me what hurts me?" Weary-eyed Peter looked at Ivan: "How do I know what hurts you?" Ivan's answer was swift: "If you don't know what hurts me, how can you say you love me?"[4]

My hope is that this book can be helpful in awakening more people to the tremendous injustice that exists in our world. I hope it is an inspiration for others so that they eventually come to experience the joy that results from having the courage to enter into the camp of the "other" and form a relationship with those who suffer oppression. It takes courage. It takes heart. The encounter can change the face of the earth.

Chapter 1

Awakening to the Hidden Violence

The United States is the wealthiest, most powerful, and technologically advanced country in the history of the world. Our abundance results from our freedoms, democracy, and blessings of God. God has truly blessed America above other nations. Why would so many flock to our shores if that wasn't true?

Haven't we been told this in many ways: that we are simply the best country to come along in history so far because of God's special favor? America does have greater wealth than any country in history and is the most powerful nation on earth. But this wealth and power are not a result of God's special blessing. They are the result of the way the powerful have organized the political, economic, legal, and military structures.

Many of us believe that poverty exists in the world because the poor are lazy, have too many children, and are just not very bright. Many have little understanding of how we have accumulated so much wealth or how the international financial institutions, with the help of the military, pave the way for multinational corporations to continue to suck the life of the poor. We do not see a link between the vast accumulated wealth in the developed countries and the hunger, disease, and deprivations of

A Cambodian girl.

all kinds in poor countries. We do not hear much about structural injustice from our pulpits. The media do not portray the brutality of the economic, political, legal, and military structures that serve us so well.

Control of the Media

Approximately fifteen hundred television stations, twelve thousand radio stations, and seventeen hundred of our newspapers are owned by corporations. The owners are Westinghouse (CBS), General Electric (NBC), Disney (ABC), and others. Corporations control the biggest networks, or 70 percent of the prime time TV markets, plus most cable channels. They also have vast holdings in radio, publishing, movie studios, and other media sectors. The mass media are aware of the needs of their advertisers, such as Nike, Budweiser, Exxon, and General Motors. Advertising is a $200 billion industry. The media know to respect the political interests of those who pay them. Corporations will not want to run their ads during exposés of pollution by multinational corporations in Third World countries, abuse suffered by workers in Central America, working conditions of children who supply products for our home, unfair treatment of women who sew our clothing, exposure to pesticides by workers who harvest our food, demonstrations in the Third World countries against the policies of the international financial institutions, and so on.

You might expect fair treatment of these subjects on PBS. You might be surprised. Consider these facts:

* During an eight-month period, only 6 percent of the guests invited to discuss environmental issues on PBS's *News Hour* represented environmental groups. Other guests were government or industry representatives.

* During a six-month period, only 3 percent of the sources quoted on public television's economics coverage represented labor, consumer, or public interest groups.

* During an eight-month period, virtually all of the sources for stories on Central America on PBS's *News Hour* were former or current officials of the U.S. government or U.S.-allied governments rather than Central American human rights activists, labor representatives, environmentalists, or other Central American citizens.[1]

There are literally hundreds of millions of stories that can be told about how people suffer horrible tragedies due to injustice. We would respond to their suffering if we were bombarded with their stories and the stories of the many heroes and heroines who are rescuing the sick, hungry and abandoned. We would respond if we knew the people who suffer so much and if we knew of the joy experienced by those heroes. We would respond also if we were shown the connection between how they suffer and the policies of the international financial institutions that force them to work in the garbage dumps and to die of malnutrition.

Guatemala is a good example of the media's failure to inform us of violence committed on our behalf and with our help. Chris Schweitzer of the Silk Hope Catholic Worker Community has written about how we have been sheltered from many truths by the media. In "Information in the Land of Oz" he cites one example:

> During the 1980s, over 200,000 civilians were killed or disappeared in Guatemala. In 1999, the Guatemalan Historical Clarification Commission released a report revealing the U.S. government's support for killing and human rights violations. President Clinton later apologized for the United States' role. How did the mass media ignore this violence, with soldiers trained and funded by the United States leveling 662 villages after raping, torturing, and killing the residents?
>
> The U.S. government has worked hard for the last 100 years to maintain pro-business governments in Latin America. U.S. corporations, such as Goodyear, RJ Reynolds, Del Monte, United Brands, US Steel, Phillip-Morris, and others were and still are very vested in the cheap labor, natural resources, and limited human and labor rights offered by Latin American governments. Corporations and governments in this country need to keep the public in the dark about the violence that the U.S. government supports. If the majority of U.S. citizens discovered that thousands of nonviolent, often church-based, teachers and organizers were being killed in Guatemala with the help of U.S. tax dollars, it is likely that a public outcry demanding an end to the government-supported oppression in Latin America would have resulted.[2]

U.S. Aid to Poor Countries

The media have led us to believe that the United States is the most generous nation in the world. One study found that two-thirds of U.S. citizens thought that the United States is the most generous when it comes to giving foreign aid to poor countries.[3] An editorial in the *New York Times* questioned: "Are we stingy?" The *Times* answered "Yes," referencing a poll that showed that most Americans believed that the United States spends 24 percent of its budget on aid to poor countries. It actually spends well under a quarter of 1 percent.

After the Second World War, we gave 2.79 percent of our Gross National Income (GNI) to rebuild Europe. By 1960, we were giving 0.52 percent of our GNI in foreign aid. By 2004, it was 0.16 percent. This puts the United States next to last on the list of developed countries and their contributions of humanitarian aid to poor countries, according to data published by the Organization of Economic Cooperation and Development (see the chart on the following page).

In terms of total dollars, Japan gave the most foreign aid from 1992 to 2000. In 2001, the United States reclaimed its position of first in terms of donor aid. We were in first place mainly due to the depreciation of the yen and our grant of $600 million to Pakistan for security purposes after 9/11. However, in terms of foreign aid as a percentage of GNI, the United States is actually next to last among Western donors. How did most of us come to accept the lie that we are the most generous nation in the world? It has been told to us over and over again on TV and radio and by politicians and TV pundits.[4]

How the stories are shaped and where they are placed are crucial to the impact. Much of what is reported in this book has been reported in the media in the United States. But you have to read very carefully. For example, a front-page headline

Official Development Assistance (ODA) as percent of Gross National Income (GNI) in 2004

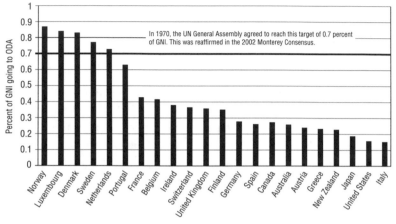

In 1970, the UN General Assembly agreed to reach this target of 0.7 percent of GNI. This was reaffirmed in the 2002 Monterey Consensus.

Source: Organization for Economic Cooperation and Development, 2005

in the *Philadelphia Inquirer* said that President Aristide of Haiti was mentally unbalanced and had been hospitalized in Montreal. This headline was published just days prior to a Congressional vote on U.S. support for Haiti. Two weeks after the vote, there was a short story on page 14 saying that the CIA had fabricated the false report and that Aristide had never been treated for mental illness as reported. Why was there no headline about how the CIA purposely lied to the American people and Congress to manipulate the politics of the poorest country in our hemisphere?

Another example is torture in Iraq. The media courageously reported on the horrors of torture inflicted on Iraqis by our soldiers. The government contended that these were isolated incidents not sanctioned by higher command. The media did a fairly good job in trying to connect the dots to shed light on the denials of higher-ups. But did they give us the whole story?

In chapter 6, you will read that in the 1950s and 1960s, the CIA paid for research to be performed in psychology departments in a half dozen universities in order to determine the most effective torture techniques. Manuals were developed by the CIA and distributed to teach the techniques that were used in Vietnam and in Latin America in the 1980s and 1990s. The same techniques were used in Abu Ghraib and Guantanamo. Yet the only place I learned of the decades-long systematic policy of torture supported by our government was in the *National Catholic Reporter* and in *Disturbing the Peace* by James Hodge and Linda Cooper. The major media never really connected the dots. It is not because they were unaware of the manuals and reporting in publications such as the *National Catholic Reporter,* as you will see in chapter 6. Two recently published books, *Torture: Religious Ethics and National Security* by John Perry and *Truth, Torture, and the American Way* by Jennifer Harbury, have also documented decades of a systematic policy of torture, apparently authored and sanctioned by the CIA. Yet the media present the issue as if there are two sides to the story, giving some credence to the government's position that the problem was low-level people who acted in violation of U.S. policy.

How and where information is presented and what parts of the story are left out have a tremendous impact on the reader or viewer. The news and commercials are effective in shaping our values. They are created by very bright people who know how to get our attention and influence our wants and needs. We human beings can be counted on to seek pleasure and avoid pain. Instinctively, we fear danger and seek safety and comfort. The TV commercial writers know how to hook us and then they reel us in. If we watch enough TV, the commercials will program quite a few of us to want what the sponsors want us to want. Many of us want pain relievers, fashionable cars, Bud and Coke, and vacations to the Caribbean. We want to look younger, to lose weight, and to buy gadgets of all kinds to save time and to make life easier. While America is the richest nation in history, many feel that they do not have enough. The commercials get us going to the malls, to the sports stadiums, and to the movies they push. We fly on airlines, eat in restaurants, and buy the clothes pushed by the commercials. The ads really do work.

Jane Eisner reported in the *Philadelphia Inquirer* (September 12, 2004), on the "commercialization of childhood." Research found that brand-name messages have pervaded the classrooms and the bedrooms of children. The typical first grader can name two hundred brands and acquires an average of seventy new toys a year. American children view an estimated forty thousand commercials annually. Teen purchasing power has risen so rapidly that teenagers spend, on average, one hundred dollars a week. Commercials now shape their parents' consumer habits to such an extent that one industry estimate says 67 percent of car purchases are influenced by children.

Corporations are driven to sell better quality products at the lowest price in order to maximize profit, to provide shareholders with a good return, and to expand. Advertising is essential to create wants. It aims at our values. It smothers our spiritual values. Detachment is a fundamental step on the path to spiritual awakening and growth. The media keep us wanting and spiritually sleepy so that we do not "see" very well.

Catholic social teaching throughout the twentieth century condemned unbridled capitalism and unregulated competition and stressed the rights of workers to organize and be paid a just wage. It condemned sinful structures that oppress and take advantage of the poor. It called for a transformation of society. But you will not hear much about structural injustice and institutionalized violence and the need to transform society from those who benefit the most from the inequities.

Chapter 2

Neocolonialism — The Search for the Most Desperate Workers

During the period of colonialism Great Britain, France, Italy, Spain, and other European powers sent soldiers to Asia, Africa, and the Americas in order to dominate and exploit resources, labor, and food. By use of guns and slavery, they established bases with political, economic, and military control over countries that then became their colonies. Today, the same powerful nations dominate the political and economic policies of the same weaker nations. This new era is sometimes referred to as neocolonialism. It is carried out by the G8, the eight most powerful countries, the United States, Great Britain, Canada, France, Germany, Italy, Spain, and Russia.

Neocolonialism accomplishes through international financial institutions what colonialism accomplished through force. Instead of sending troops, the powerful support the less developed countries' (LDCs') military to maintain the status quo while corporations take advantage of their natural resources and their workers through outsourcing. Outsourcing involves setting up subsidiary companies or contracting with companies in LDCs to supply particular goods and services to developed countries.

In the 1980s and 1990s, a major shift began when manufacturers began in earnest to relocate from the rich northern countries to the poor southern countries in search of the most vulnerable and desperate workers.

17

Going South — The Race to the Bottom

Labor costs are a significant part of production costs. In order to compete, many companies look for workers willing to work for the lowest wages. The most desperate will work for the lowest rate.

In the United States during the 1960s and 1970s, many unionized jobs were relocated from northern states to southern states to avoid unions and to pay lower wages. They then went farther south to Mexico and Central America. Now they are going from Mexico to Asia. In order to be competitive, companies are forced to lower their costs. If they don't, their profit and stock values will go down. They won't be around unless they join the search for the most desperate workers.

The chairs of the corporate boards of directors and CEOs know that the relatively high cost of labor in the United States is related to the justice built into our system. For example:

+ child labor laws
+ minimum wage laws
+ occupational safety and health laws
+ environmental protection laws
+ the right to organize labor unions
+ equal pay for men and women
+ time and a half for overtime (over forty hours a week)
+ age discrimination laws
+ Americans with Disabilities Act
+ civil rights protection for race and creed
+ workers' compensation laws
+ unemployment benefits
+ Social Security disability benefits

They are also keenly aware of the costs associated with compliance with both labor and environmental protection laws. So in order to be competitive and to increase profit, many lay off American workers and relocate to countries where they can legally get away with paying starvation wages, using child labor, requiring long working hours, ignoring hazards, firing older workers without cause, paying women less than men, not promoting women, repressing unions, and so on. It is just good business to squeeze and exploit the poorest, most desperate workers to the greatest degree. In fact, it is an imperative for survival if you want to earn as much as your competitors. So thousands of American companies abandon millions of American workers so they do not have to bother with the cost of justice in our system.

Adam Smith taught that in the capitalistic system there is an "invisible hand" that, through the profit motive and free markets, drives the economy to the most efficient outcomes. That is, giving industry decision makers the freedom to maximize profits without the interference of government regulation is the best way to produce the most for the largest number of people. But if you gather a group of grade school children around a table with lots of toys on it and ask them to design the best way to get the most toys to the most children, they would see a problem with just giving everybody the freedom of trying to get the most for themselves. They would know that the big guys would get the most and the little guys would probably get hurt in the struggle.

In the 1960s in Economics 101, students debated the notion of whether or not "what is good for General Motors is good for America." That is what Charlie Wilson, the CEO of General Motors, said. Now General Motors has been closing factories in the United States and opening them abroad. GM's newest plants are going up in Argentina, Poland, China, and Thailand. GM used to be the largest employer in the United States. Today it is the largest employer in Mexico, where it has built fifty plants in twenty years. In 1996, the United States shipped 46,000 cars to Mexico, and Mexico sent 550,000 cars to the United States.

In 1985, GE employed 243,000 workers. Ten years later, that number was down to 150,000. IBM lopped off half its U.S. workforce in the past decade. For the past ten years, there has been a steady stream of companies firing U.S. workers and going south. The products come north.

- 83 percent of all clothing purchased in the U.S. is made in poor countries.

- 95 percent of shoes, sneakers, sporting goods, and computers are made in poor countries ($170 billion each year).

- 80 percent of toys are made in China ($29.4 billion each year).[1]

- 100 percent of all televisions sold in the United States are produced in poor countries.

- 80 percent of all electronics are made in poor countries.[2]

Campesinos in Mexico, El Salvador, Honduras, and other Central American countries supply us with coffee, cocoa, bananas, sugar, cotton, pineapples, apples, grapes, pears, and so on. Metals extracted from mines in Bolivia, Peru, and Chile (copper, tin, lead, tungsten) are formed in foundries in Mexico to become components used in our cars. Our carpets come from India, Pakistan, and Bangladesh and may be made by child labor. Young boys work as slaves in the Ivory Coast in Africa and supply cocoa used in our chocolate. Computer parts and televisions come from India; teak furniture from Honduras; rubber from Thailand; radios from Taiwan; meat, tuna, bananas, and pineapples from the Philippines; sugar from the Dominican Republic; and so on. Go to your closet. You will see labels from

Latin America and Asia. Go to your malls. You will see that almost everything comes from the labor of poor people from poor countries. It is true that manufacturing and farming for exports provide employment in the developing countries. However, the essential question is whether it is a fair deal. The National Labor Committee has researched this question.

Raising Awareness

The National Labor Committee has played a major role in bringing attention to the exploitation of poor workers. The committee is a coalition of labor unions, religious organizations, students, human rights activists, civil rights activists, women's organizations, and community organizations who believe that worker rights are fundamental human rights. Coalition members include the United Methodist Church Women's Division, the People of Faith Network, the United Steel Workers of America, the United Students Against Sweatshops, TransAfrica, the New York Public Interest Research Group, and the Progressive National Baptist Convention. The following comes from their research:

> **Wal-Mart.** When you purchase a toy at Wal-Mart, do you ever imagine teenage women in China working from 7:30 a.m. to 2 a.m., eighteen and a half hours a day, seven days a week, in 104 degree temperatures, handling toxic chemicals with their bare hands, and paid as little as thirteen cents an hour? One woman described how she felt at the end of her shift at 2 a.m. — her vision blurred, eyes watery, sick to her stomach, her back aching, her fingers cut and bleeding from the sharp metal edges of the die-cast toy cars she had painted for Mattel.
>
> In the Chun Shi factory in China, Wal-Mart suppliers were forced to work from 7 a.m. to 11 p.m., sixteen hours

© Jared C. Benedict

a day, thirty days a month, for an average wage of just *three cents an hour!* And they were the "lucky ones." Forty-six percent of the workers were held as indentured servants and actually owed the company money. When workers asked for their rights, they were beaten, and eight hundred were fired.

Wal-Mart responded by claiming that they had never heard of the factory, let alone produced goods there. However, under pressure, Wal-Mart vice-president Jay Allen had to admit that Wal-Mart lied because they felt "defensive" about the sweatshop issue.

Alcoa. Can you imagine that Alcoa workers in Mexico, in the high-tech factories making auto parts for export to the U.S., live in dirt-floor cardboard huts and sell their blood twice a week in order to survive?

The U.S. Government. The U.S. government formed a joint venture with the military dictators in Myanmar

(Burma) to establish a factory to make clothing. The workers were paid just seven cents an hour — three dollars and twenty-three cents a week. Workers who dare to speak up for their rights are subjected to imprisonment and torture.

Harvard University. Women in Bangladesh are paid 1.6 cents for each $17 Harvard cap they sew. Their wages come to just one-tenth of 1 percent of the retail price. U.S. Custom records show that the cap is valued at $1.23 when it enters the United States. Then Harvard marks it up 1,300 percent.

Nike. Nike workers in Indonesia earn $4.76 a day, or a total of $811 a year. Labor for a pair of basketball shoes that retail for $149.50 costs Nike $1.50, 1 percent of the retail price. Nike's total revenue for 1997 was $9.19 billion, with a profit of $795.8 million. CEO Bill Knight's fourth-quarter dividend earnings were $80 million.

Disney in Bangladesh. Young women sewing Disney shirts are forced to work fifteen hours a day, seven days a week. They are paid five cents for each $17.99 shirt they sew. They are beaten, punched, and slapped, denied maternity leave and benefits. When they reach twenty-five to thirty years of age, they are fired and replaced by younger girls. In a five-year period, Michael Eisner, the CEO of Disney, paid himself $667 million, about $63,000 an hour. A worker in Bangladesh, paid twelve cents an hour to sew Disney garments, would have to work 210 years to earn what Eisner does in one hour.[3]

Hazards Facing Women in Developing Countries

A young woman from American Samoa testified before Congress on November 28, 2001, about the Daewoosa factory, which supplied clothing for Wal-Mart and other retailers:

There were three pregnant women among us. Mr. Lee demanded that they undergo abortions. He fired them when they refused. . . . At the workplace, Mr. Lee regularly groped and kissed female workers in front of everyone. . . . Mr. Lee used big American Samoan guards to terrorize us. On November 28, 2000, there was a dispute between a supervisor and a female worker. Mr. Lee ordered the supervisor: "If you beat her to death, I will take the blame." The supervisor dragged the female out. Other workers came to her rescue. The American Samoan guards, already holding sticks and scissors, jumped in and beat us. Everyone was frightened. We ran for our lives. . . . Ms. Quyen was held by her arms on two sides by the guards. A third guard thrust a pointed stick into her eye. She has now lost that eye. . . . A guard beat a male worker with a stick, breaking his front teeth and bloodying his mouth. Another male worker was pinned to the floor and repeatedly beaten at the temple, his blood spilling all over the floor.

Garment workers at the Pantex factory in Bangladesh protested ten-cents-an-hour wages, fifteen-hour shifts for seven days a week. They blocked the gate at 5 a.m. on November 3, 2003. The owner called the police who, without warning, opened fire, killing seven workers. The police went on a rampage, beating and seriously injuring 151 workers. A thirteen-year-old girl was shot in the stomach. Police then roped the young women together, using cords to bind their wrists and ankles as if they were animals (see the photo on p. 70).[4]

In Bangladesh, young women told the National Labor Committee that if their wages were raised to thirty cents an hour, they would be able to feed themselves and their children at least one good meal a day. This would raise them from desperation to poverty.

If workers in poor countries were paid fair wages, had safe and healthy working conditions, and had the right to health care and other protections against discrimination and abuse, prices in the United States would be higher. But justice requires a fair distribution of money.

Catholic social teaching has long supported workers' rights to organize and to earn a just wage. From Pope Leo XIII in *Rerum Novarum* to Pope Benedict XVI, the teaching of the popes has been to recognize the importance of combating injustice and the transformation of society. Pope Pius XI condemned capitalism and unregulated competition and affirmed the church's right and duty to address workers' rights to a just wage and to organize. Pope John XXIII emphasized in *Peace on Earth* (1963) the right to organize and to a just wage. Pope Paul VI's encyclical letter *The Development of Peoples* (1967) responded to the cries of the world's poor, addressing the structural dimensions of global injustice and the need for pastoral action to fight injustice. He strongly criticized the desire for profit and the thirst for power, calling them "structures of sin." Pope Benedict XVI has written about the need for structural transformation to achieve social justice. Despite these teachings, many believe that the poor should be grateful because any job is better than no job at all.

Isn't a Low-Paying Job Better Than No Job at All?

Poor workers interviewed by human rights activists invariably say that they don't want to lose their job. A person paid starvation wages while suffering harassment and abuse does not choose unemployment instead. In countries with thousands of desperately poor people, there is a demand for jobs, even those paying starvation wages. But that doesn't mean it is just to pay starvation wages.

In the United States, we have about 32 million teenagers who spend over $155 billion a year ($110 a month) on clothing alone. It is not just that desperately poor teenagers have to sacrifice so much to clothe the relatively wealthy teenagers in developed countries.

The Church World Service helps us to see that almost everything we use is brought to us by workers in developing countries (see the facing page). We have more because they have so little.

We can live half awake or in denial of the tremendous suffering of the people who toil to bring us our food, clothing, and almost all our consumer goods. We can try to overlook the connection and to ignore Lazarus. Or we can face it with courage and humility and ask for the grace to hear the cry of the poor and to be shown how we can do our part.

> Before you finish eating breakfast this morning, you've depended on more than half the world. This is the way our universe is structured.... We aren't going to have peace on earth until we recognize this basic fact of the interrelated structure of all reality.
>
> — *Martin Luther King Jr.*

Teak from Honduras where in rural villages people earn an average of six dollars a month.

Bananas, tuna and meat from Somalia, with one of the greatest food shortages in the world.

Baseball and glove from Haiti, poorest nation in the Western hemisphere where wages are 18 cents an hour.

Assembled in Taiwan. Workers earn less than 25 cents an hour.

Bastnaesite from Burundl. Life expectancy is 42 years.

Pineapple from Philippines. One-half of children under four have severe protein deficiency.

Coffee from Guatemala. Two-thirds of population has annual income of $42.

Other common items supplied by third-world nations: tea from Bangladesh; copper wiring from Chile; aluminum from Jamaica; tin from Malaysia; dog food from fishmeal from Peru; cork (for bulletin board) from Algeria; natural gas from Mexico.

Modified with permission of
Church World Services
P.O. Box 968
Elkhart, Indiana 46515
1-800-297-1516

Chapter 3

International Financial Institutions — Instruments of Development or Violence?

Neocolonialism is supported by the major international financial institutions (the International Monetary Fund, the World Bank, the World Trade Organization) controlled by the powerful and wealthy. The World Bank supplies the money, and the IMF and the World Trade Organization set the rules. The philosophy that supports neocolonialism is neoliberalism, that is, a vision according to which global corporations can operate without restrictions from government regulations. The international financial institutions pave the way for stable, safe investments for transnational corporations by establishing financial and legal arrangements between the less developed countries (LDCs) and themselves. This has resulted in more and more products and food being exported to the rich countries and in growing inequity and indebtedness within the LDCs. Some LDCs pay up to 40 percent of their total tax revenue just for the annual interest on their debt.

In the 1960s, the U.S. government spent more than it earned to support the war in Vietnam and then made up for it by printing more dollars. The value of the dollar fell. The oil-producing nations, whose oil was priced in dollars, lost a lot of money. So in 1973, they quadrupled their prices. This resulted in the oil-export nations making huge deposits in Western banks. With so much money available for loans, interest rates plummeted. The banks then faced a crisis. They decided to stop the slide by encouraging the LDCs to take out loans. They assumed that the loans were safe because entire nations would not go bankrupt.

As a result, the LDCs began accepting more loans and got deeper in debt. During the 1980s, the international financial institutions began requiring debtor nations to institute structural adjustment programs (SAPs), that is, programs that require the indebted countries to restructure their economies in ways that ensured that the LDCs would continue to supply cheap goods to the developed countries. Under the SAPs more and more goods come from the LDCs to the developed countries, and the debt of the LDCs continues to grow. Essentially, the poor work to feed and supply goods to the rich. It is an old story.

The International Monetary Fund

The International Monetary Fund was established in 1945 to promote the health of the world economy. It is headquartered in Washington, DC, and is governed by 184 member countries. The IMF is the central institution of the International Monetary System, that is, the system of international payments and exchange rates among national currencies that enables business to take place between countries. It was established to promote international monetary cooperation, exchange stability, and orderly exchange arrangements; to foster economic growth and high levels of employment; and to provide temporary financial assistance to countries to help ease balance of payment adjustments. While the World Bank is concerned mainly with long-term development, poverty reduction measures, project funding, and structural adjustment, the IMF's focus is mainly on short-term stabilization.

World Bank

The World Bank is an association of five institutions owned by 184 member countries. It is run like a cooperative with its member countries as shareholders. The United States is the largest with 16.41 percent of the votes, followed by Japan (7.87 percent), Germany (4.49 percent), the United Kingdom (4.31 percent), and France (4.30 percent). The rest of the shares are divided among the other member countries. The World Bank began to lend money to developing countries in 1948. With its headquarters in Washington, it employs approximately ten thousand development professionals and has offices in 109 countries.

The World Bank makes loans at low or market interest rates based on a country's ability to repay. The Bank also provides grants, interest-free loans, and technical assistance. It is currently involved in more than eighteen hundred projects in virtually every sector of every developing country. It seeks to maximize profit through lending money and promoting foreign private investment. Its goal is to promote long-range balanced growth of international trade. In the early 1980s it began to require the LDCs to comply with certain "conditions" before receiving further assistance. It began to implement structural adjustment policies.

Structural Adjustment Policies — 1980

Money is the lifeblood of our economic system. The indebted countries need money to build their infrastructure. That is, they need roads, dams, electrical power, airports, telecommunications, ports, and vocational-technical training of workers so that multinational corporations find a good environment for investment. The indebted countries also need money to restructure and repay their debts. Money is essential.

In the 1980s, the World Bank went beyond just lending for projects like roads and dams to providing broad-based support in the form of structural adjustment loans. These loans had to be approved by the IMF, which imposed "conditions" on the loans.

In order for an indebted country to be eligible for further loans and grants, it had to make certain "adjustments" to its political and economic structures. According to the international financial institutions the adjustments are intended to promote development. They are designed to make it easier for an indebted country to pay its debts while increasing exports, that is, agricultural products and goods primarily manufactured by subsidiaries of multinational corporations or their "outsourcing" companies. In essence, the structural adjustment program requires the indebted country to export more and to spend less. The indebted country must usually agree to do some or all of the following:

+ deregulate prices and currency

+ cut spending in health, education, sanitation, agriculture, and other services

+ privatize state-owned industries

+ eliminate trade barriers

+ reorient the economy to modernize the export of crops such as coffee, cocoa, bananas, sugar, peanut

+ deregulate the labor market, that is, make it easier for employers to hire and fire and have greater control over cheaper labor.

If the indebted country complies with the structural adjustment requirements, it gives the green light to foreign investors, commercial banking institutions, and bilateral donors of foreign aid to invest in the country. If the indebted country refuses to implement the structural adjustment policies, it will be refused loans and funding from outside sources. Countries that refuse to go along or refuse to repay their loans will face disaster as a result of economic isolation. The three most devastating of the structural adjustment policies of the IMF are devaluation of the currency, cuts in government spending, and privatization.

Devaluation of the Currency

As a precondition to negotiation of a structural adjustment loan, currency devaluation is often required. The rate of exchange regulates the real prices paid to direct purchasers as well as the real value of wages. The cost of labor goes down and the cost of products is cheaper. That is, the dollar can buy more. Theoretically, this is good for the economy of the poor country because there will be a greater demand for exported goods. However, the social impact of the IMF-sponsored devaluation is usually brutal and immediate. Overnight the prices of food, drugs, fuel, public services, and many other products increase sometimes 30 to 50 percent. In poor countries high school students, taxi drivers, and people with no formal education come to realize that prices rise after the visits by IMF representatives are reported in the newspapers. Most people in the United States have no idea how this system works. Poor people know all about it because of the way it impacts their lives. The prices of everything go up.[1] When I lived in Peru there were periodic devaluations of the Peruvian currency, the *sole*. I was paid in dollars, so with each devaluation I exchanged my dollars for more Peruvian *soles*. The purchasing power of the dollar increased. However, the Peruvian people's purchasing power diminished, pushing some over the edge.

Approximately half of the world's population, over 3 billion people, live on less than two dollars a day. It is hard for us to imagine living on such a small sum. Try to imagine the anguish felt by millions of people in poor countries when prices go up. People become desperate. Sometimes children are taken out of school and forced to work at the garbage dump or in the business district peddling lottery tickets, shining shoes, or selling food made by their mother. Some women resort to prostitution to survive. Some parents sell their children to people who say the child will work in a restaurant or factory. Sometimes they end up in the sex trade.

Increases in the cost of transportation can be devastating. For example, workers living in a poor area may take three buses to get to work. With devaluation, transportation costs can go up five cents for each bus fare. So the cost to get to the job and back can go up thirty cents a day or more. If the workers were already living on less than a dollar a day, as over 1 billion people do, the devaluation can push them over the edge. It may now be better for them to go to the local garbage dump to collect paper, bottles, metal, and plastic to sell for recycling. They may be able to find food at the dump.

Cuts in Government Spending

Cuts in government spending give governments more money to repay their loans. Cuts often result in significant increases in unemployment as government workers are fired. For example, cuts in spending meant that in Bolivia, Ecuador, Honduras, the Dominican Republic and Venezuela, 20 to 40 percent of public officials lost their jobs and were living below the poverty threshold.[2]

The poorest of the poor suffer the most when the government cuts money for essential services. Cuts to ministries of health particularly affect the poor. Like in many other countries, in Peru the sick must pay for food and medicine in public hospitals. They must bring their own sheets. People without the money for medicine, food, or sheets suffer their illness at home.

The weak suffer the most, and the weakest are always the children. Every week in the developing world two hundred thousand children under the age of five die of disease.[3] It is not unusual for children to die for lack of antibiotics that would cost less than ten dollars.

A grandmother from a poor section of Mexico City saw the collapse of the public health system as a result of cuts in government spending. She recounted: "They operated on my husband six months ago. He paid social security all of his life, but they told him he had to buy his medicine privately and provide two liters of blood — my son had to give it. All they give you is penicillin for everything — it's the magic ingredient!"[4]

In one Nicaraguan town a notice on the health center's grimy wall reads: "Anyone coming for an injection must bring their own syringe, elastoplast, gauze, and bandages. Attention is free. Thank you."[5]

Cuts to ministries of education mean that teachers' salaries are cut, class size increases, and teachers are fired. Teachers' salaries may be cut to as low as $70 a month. It is impossible for a family to live on $70 a month in most poor countries. Stores in the poor areas around Lima sell much more animal feed than the chickens eat. People are eating animal feed.

When workers lose their jobs, many then enter the "informal market." In Peru and Haiti, for example, more than 70 percent of the workers work in the "informal market." Formal workers work for the government or companies and receive periodic payment for their work. Informal workers do whatever they can to survive. There is no unemployment insurance, welfare, or food stamps. So the unemployed often try to sell something in the market. Or they perform services for middle- or upper-class people: shine shoes, cut grass, or work as maids.

Privatization

The World Bank will demand that the indebted country sell some or most of the government-owned industry. It is not unusual for an indebted country to own basic industries like mines, refineries, airlines, banks, sugar mills, power plants, telephone companies, or steel mills. The IMF believes that these companies will be more efficient if they are run by businessmen rather than government employees, so they require the government to sell them. Often the nationally owned company is sold to a multinational corporation. The state-owned monopolies then become monopolies wholly owned by foreigners.

One example of privatization is the Bolivian Water Company. In 1999, the Bechtel Corporation was given a forty-year lease to supply water to Bolivia. Within a week of taking over, it tripled water prices. Families suddenly faced monthly bills of more than twenty dollars to be paid from earnings of less than one hundred dollars a month. Because of protests, martial law was declared. The contract was canceled. However, Bechtel sued the Bolivian government for $25 million for breach of contract.[6]

Finally, privatization often results in significant unemployment as the workforce is reduced by the new owner.

World Trade Organization

In 1995, the World Trade Organization (WTO) replaced the General Agreement on Tariffs and Trades (GATT). It now has 120 members. It deals with the rules of trade between nations at a global or near-global level. It operates a system of trade rules and serves as a forum for governments to negotiate trade agreements and to settle trade disputes. At its heart are the WTO agreements, negotiated and signed by the majority of the world's trading nations. These documents provide the legal ground rules for international commerce. They are essentially contracts, binding governments to keep trade policies within agreed limits.

The World Trade Organization is concerned not only with cutting trade barriers and tariffs. It also sets rules for domestic food safety standards, environmental and product safety rules, service-sector regulations, investment and development policy, intellectual property standards, government procurement rules, and more. These rules were written under the influence of the world's largest multinational corporations; five hundred U.S. corporations were U.S. government advisors. The purpose of the rules is to facilitate global corporations' competition for wealth. Global corporations are, of course, concerned with their economic self-interests not the interest of any particular country or the needs of any particular people. The corporations are not designed or intended to benefit workers or to reduce poverty. The rules facilitate the growth of corporations without interference from government regulation. Jeff Faux in *The Global Class War* reports:

> The WTO restricts governments' ability to regulate the behavior of multinational businesses and weakens the public sector's capacity to provide protection and services for its citizens. The core principle of the WTO is not free trade among sovereign states. It is, as Peter Sutherland, GATT Director, said in 1994, that in every state, "governments should interfere in the conduct of the economy as little as possible."
>
> The WTO forbids all governments to condition foreign investments on the purchase of supplies from domestic businesses or to prohibit the entry of certain products that its scientists deem unsafe or its people believe immoral (for example, produced with child labor). The WTO protects patent monopolies of multinational corporations and prohibits laws protecting workers and the environment or public health that interfere with the freedom of corporations to invest, buy, and sell.... Both NAFTA and the

WTO ... set limits on the behavior of government; define rights of citizenship; establish a judicial system to interpret its own text in the case of conflicts; and provide for enforcement of the courts' decisions. The "nullification and impairment" section of the WTO allows corporations to challenge the laws of any country that can be shown to impair the benefits that the corporation could expect to receive under the WTO. Using this provision, the government of Canada, on behalf of its asbestos industry, has brought suit against France for its domestic ban on the use of asbestos.[7]

It is no wonder so many people in the LDCs, as well as in the developed countries, have demonstrated against the WTO and regional trade agreements such as the North American Free Trade Agreement (NAFTA), the Central American Free Trade Agreement (CAFTA), and the Free Trade Agreement of the Americas (FTAA). Ralph Nader challenged any member of Congress to read the twenty-five thousand pages of the World Trade Agreement and then answer ten questions posed by an independent journalist. Nader offered to give $10,000 to the member's favorite charity if he or she answered the ten questions correctly. The only representative who took up his offer was Senator Hank Brown, a Republican from Colorado. He was going to vote for the WTO, but after scoring 100 percent on the test he decided to vote against it saying: "Anyone who thinks this agreement expands free trade has not read it."[8]

Critics of the policies of the World Trade Organization and the regional trade organizations include small farmers in both the LDCs and the developed countries and activists such as environmentalists, labor representatives, public health professionals, occupational safety and health professionals, consumer rights advocates, human rights advocates, and clergy who serve the poor. They are concerned about environmental protection, conservation, food and public safety, access to essential public services, food security, public health, worker safety, access to medicine, jobs, livelihood, economic development, and human and labor rights. They are concerned that the multinational corporations that exercise control over government officials are imposing rules that undermine democracy.

Chapter 4

How the Poor Suffer

Come away, O human child!
To the waters and the wild
With a faery, hand in hand
For the world's more full of weeping
than you can understand.
— William Butler Yeats, "The Stolen Child"

Working at the Garbage Dump

When structural adjustment programs are implemented, the poorest of the poor suffer the most. Price increases due to devaluation devastate people who are already struggling every day for food to survive. Cuts in government health care services can be life threatening for people with no other access to health care. Unemployment due to privatization can force families into desperate poverty.

I first realized the horrors faced by families at the garbage dumps when I was asked by the International Labor Organization of the United Nations to research the occupational hazards faced by informal workers. At the garbage dump informal workers collect paper, bottles, metal, and plastic to sell. The paper is sold to others who sell it to paper mills. The glass goes to glass container manufacturers. The metal goes to foundries, and the plastic is melted and reformed again into new plastic products.

39

P. J. Gallagher

Boy working in a dump in Guatemala City.

The most dangerous of informal work is performed by women and children at the garbage dumps throughout developing countries. While collecting products to be recycled, they are exposed to biological waste from hospitals, human waste, industrial waste from factories, sharp glass, and metal. They also face the risk of fires and explosions when the methane gas that forms in the decaying garbage is disturbed by bulldozers. And they can be run over by bulldozers. Father Don Vettese, a Jesuit priest, visited a garbage dump in Mexico:

> It was the way I would envision hell. Toddlers playing in raw sewage, children fighting vultures for scraps of meat, people with open sores and missing limbs looking through piles of garbage for plastic they could sell to recycle for a few pesos. The living conditions were so appalling that I became physically ill. It was unforgettable heat, stench,

birds larger than the children, the adults with nothing but hopelessness in their eyes.[1]

Father Vettese saw small children covered with cardboard to keep the vultures from pecking at them. And he saw Lucia.

Lucia's lined face and lifeless expression speaks of many years of deprivation. She is only twenty-one, hardly a senior citizen. An infant is wrapped in rags in a blanket strapped on her back, and a thin little girl stands in her shadow. Armed with two sacks, Lucia is ready for the day. In one sack will go recyclables — plastic, tin, whatever she can sell; and the other, scraps of food for her family's meal.[2]

The dump in Lima is appalling. The stench is horrible. There are no showers. There is little water to wash with or to drink. Diarrhea, worms, and fever flourish. No one can afford health care. People usually eat only once a day; twice is considered a good day. On a bad day, they eat from the garbage. Many sniff glue, including the children. Most families are headed by single women. Abortion among desperately poor women is common.

The workers are mostly boys from five to fifteen years old. There are some girls. And there are toddlers who just sit nearby while their older brothers or sisters work. Their mothers may be working in the business district selling food or anything they can.

Children Who Live and Work on the Streets

UNICEF estimates that in Latin America 90 million children, or almost one-half of all children on the continent, live in poverty. It reports that there are 100 million street children in the world, of whom half are found in Latin America.[3] Street children live, work, and sleep on the streets and often lack regular contact with their families. The increase in the number of street children over the last decade has been massive — an eightfold increase in Tegucigalpa, Honduras, alone.

There are tens of millions of children who live and work on the streets of the major cities of Asia, Africa, and Latin America. Implementation of structural adjustment programs forces some of the poorest of families to take their children out of school and send them to work or beg in the business district. Their parents send them to the streets because they cannot afford to do otherwise. The children meet gangs of other children and may get involved in stealing and sniffing glue. Some go home to have their earnings taken by an alcoholic father who beats them. Many decide not to go home. They find it better in the streets.

> I left home when I was nine. I lived in Otay. They [the other boys] invited me to take drugs and at first I didn't want to but then I wanted to see what it felt like. I slept in the streets. I lay down anywhere. I am fourteen now and I've got to like being in the streets.... Some clients come and look for us when we're in the center playing on the machines.... That's where the people go to find us. If you like the price, you go, if not, you don't.... Some offer you ten dollars to go to their home, but you say thirty or it's not on....   — Fourteen-year-old boy, Tijuana, Mexico [4]

The older boys abuse the younger ones. Men abuse the boys and girls. The girls are particularly vulnerable. The children sleep in doorways, in alleys, under bridges, and in sewers.

Owners of jewelry shops, dress shops, and restaurants do not want these children hanging around because they scare customers. The children are dirty, some steal, and when they are fifteen or sixteen years old, they can be very dangerous. They may be criminally insane from physical or sexual abuse and drugs. So groups of children are sometimes gathered into vans, taken out of town, and shot. Hundreds have been killed in Bogotá, Rio de Janeiro, and other cities. The children know what is happening.

The following was reported in *LatinAmerica Press* in 1990:

> Hundreds of children are assassinated by death squads and tortured by police in Brazilian cities in order to "clean the streets," according to a recent Amnesty International report.... On October 6, a common grave containing the remains of 560 children was discovered in São Paulo's Don Bosco cemetery. The grave was discovered by members of a newly appointed committee established by São Paulo's mayor, who are investigating the records of the cemetery. The first unmarked grave, which contained the remains of some 1,400 people, was uncovered two months ago. Sociologist Herbert de Sousa, IBASE Director, said that the murder of children in Brazil "means nothing." ... In the last five years, the majority of more than one thousand children who were murdered on the streets were black males between the ages of fifteen and eighteen.... Recently, two military police officers from Pratopolis, in the central state of Minas Gerais, were accused of torturing seven children, aged eight to eleven.... According to one of the children's father, his son was tied up and dangled over the side of one of the city bridges.[5]

Thousands of children also live and work on the streets in the United States. Covenant House in New York City cares for over forty thousand children who need shelter each year. Covenant House operates shelters in New York City, Philadelphia, Atlantic City, Mexico City, Tegucigalpa, and other cities. A boy may leave home to live and work on the streets because his mother suffers an addiction supported by prostitution, and she brings her "clients" home, which he finds intolerable. Or a girl may be abused by her father or stepfather and runs away. To survive, they may sell drugs or their bodies. Covenant House workers reach out to rescue these children, to provide shelter and safety, and, if appropriate, to help them return home. In Latin America, there are many organizations, mostly religious based, who care for children who live on the streets. But there are far too few.

Sexually Exploited Children

When poor people are squeezed economically, some eventually become so desperate that they give a child away for as little as two or three hundred dollars. Some work in a restaurant or factory; others end up in the sex trade. Each year 1 million children become child prostitutes.

Antonia Pinto, who worked as a cook and procurer in a gold-mining town in the Amazon, describes the fate of young prostitutes:

> On more than ten occasions, I awoke in the morning to find the corpse of a young girl floating in the water by the barge. Nobody bothered to bury the girls. They just threw their bodies in the river to be eaten by the fish.[6]

It has also been reported that 10 to 12 million children worldwide are visited by pedophiles, and one-third of all child prostitutes in Asia are HIV-positive. According to a 1994–95 UNICEF report, Asia has an estimated 1 million child prostitutes, including an estimated 300,000 in India, 200,000 in Thailand, 100,000 in the Philippines, 40,000 in Vietnam, 30,000 in Sir Lanka, and many thousands in China. In Bogotá, Colombia, the number of prostitutes under thirteen has quintupled since 1987. Brazil now has more than 250,000 child prostitutes. In 1994, American juvenile prostitutes numbered half a million.[7]

Children are sold from Burma, Laos, and China through Bangkok to Malaysia, Singapore, Hong Kong, Japan, and to the United States, Europe, and Australia. Thousands of Nepali girls, prized for their fair skin and delicate features, as young as ten years old are sold and trafficked into the brothels of Bombay. Dinka and Nuba children from Southern Sudan are sold into Libya, where many become concubines. Men from Europe, North America, and Australia vacation regularly on the beaches of Sir Lanka, Thailand, and other Asian shores where the sex industry supplies them with girls or boys of their choice. Especially in Asia, but also in Africa, children are forced or sold into sex labor to pay off the debts of their parents. Often these debts are arranged so the children are never able to pay them off and so continue for years as sex slaves.[8]

In a book entitled *Sexually Exploited Children,* Marjorie McDermid writes of the magnitude of the horror of sexual exploitation of children and tells the sad story of a Manilan girl named Veronica.

> Anastasia Santos last saw her daughter, Veronica, a year ago, before her child was traded to a brothel for $500 by a woman who lured the girl to the city with a vague promise of work. Veronica can't leave the brothel in Manila until she earns the $500 the owner paid the brothel agent. That day may never come. She serves an average of ten men a day at four dollars per customer, but three of the four dollars are deducted for room, food and cosmetics: she must also pay the brothel owner for clothes. Today she is in debt beyond the original $500 to a pimp and has been infected with HIV. Veronica's life has ended and she is not yet twelve years old.[9]

Child prostitution and trafficking of children are linked to poverty, economic development, industrialization, increasing materialism, international tourism, and militarization. Inappropriate development policies have deprived rural people of their land and a means of survival. Forced into desperate poverty or lured by materialism, thousands of Thai villagers, for example, have chosen to sell their land or knowingly even their children to agents for a few hundred dollars.[10] In nine villages in three northern provinces, only five girls between three and sixteen years of age remained in the village. Research indicates that less than 10 percent of Thai adolescents enter prostitution willingly; 90 percent enter because of family poverty.[11]

The Effect of Debt on Families

The money that indebted countries are forced to pay to the World Bank diverts much-needed resources from investments in children, such as education and health care. Of the forty-eight least developed countries, thirty are classified as heavily indebted poor countries (HIPCs). High debt service invariably reduces expenditures for basic social services, with three results. First, less government spending on basic social services means higher costs for households. In several HIPCs, families must now pay user fees for primary education and basic health care that used to be free of charge. For the poorest families, therefore, user fees mark the end of their access to basic social services. Reduced government expenditure not only limits access but negatively affects the quality of services.

The second effect of reduced government expenditure on basic social services is to undermine the quality of the services. Schools are short-staffed and teachers are underpaid. Children lack access to books or pencils and are forced to learn in crowded classrooms with little equipment. Similarly, staffs in hospitals find themselves having to work without vaccines, drugs, or needed equipment. Sometimes hospitals are without electricity, medicine, or beds.

The third effect is that human development stagnates and may even decline. In Mozambique, for example, debt service took up about half of the central government's revenue. This worked out to roughly seven dollars per capita. The government spent less than half of this — three dollars per person — on health care. In one year, 160,000 children died before reaching the age of five. Figures from Tanzania were even more extreme. Debt service received nine times the expenditure on basic health care and four times the spending on primary education. One Tanzanian child in seven died before reaching the age of five, and 2.4 million were not in school. In Zambia, where debt service takes up one-third of the government revenue, health and education indicators deteriorated in the 1990s. Poverty and child mortality are rising; the number of children in school is declining. Yet, even in the face of deteriorating social indicators, the debt continues to be serviced.[12]

The world's attention was brought to the problem of African countries' indebtedness by the Live 8 Concert held in July of 2005 just before the meeting of the G8 in Gleneagles, Scotland. The G8 agreed to cancel $40 billion of debt of eighteen poor countries that have passed the strict economic reform monitoring process of the IMF and the World Bank's heavily indebted poor country (HIPC) initiative. As many as twenty other countries could be eligible if they complied with the required economic reforms. Is this a sign of hope for the restructuring of international financial institutions to give poor countries greater economic freedom?

News Notes, a bimonthly newsletter of the Maryknoll Office for Global Concerns, has reported on debt cancellation and comments made by concerned nongovernmental organizations. In an article entitled "Fifty Years Is Enough" it reports:

For years, debt cancellation campaigners have advocated 100 percent debt cancellation without harmful conditions. Advocates who have been critical of the June G8 deal say that not enough countries are represented and that, though it is a step forward, it is overly dependent on existing IMF conditions and the failed HIPC program. Tying conditions directly to debt cancellation in addition to the policy support instrument (PSI) could negate any potential benefits of the G8 deal.[13]

The Jubilee USA Network called the political agreement a "first step toward the amount of debt cancellation needed to end the debt crisis and eradicate global poverty," but joined other voices around the world, including Jubilee South and the African Forum and Network on Debt and Development, in criticizing the accord.[14] It also reported:

The existing debt framework, the heavily indebted poor countries (HIPC) initiative, has failed to provide a solution to the debt crisis. Designed by creditors in 1996, it dictates economic policies and extracts the maximum in debt repayments from poor countries before writing off the balance. Recent WB and IMF reports concede that the HIPC initiative has failed to provide an exit from the debt crisis that those countries face. Independent audits of these two institutions have confirmed that they can afford to write off Africa's debt completely. The fourteen African countries in the present debt cancellation proposal were not chosen because they are the poorest countries. Rather they were chosen because they've already completed the harsh HIPC program and received some debt relief, but it has proven to be insufficient to halt their further impoverishment.

The World Bank and the IMF held their annual meeting at the end of September 2005. At that time, over twenty faith-based organizations signed a letter to the World Bank to express their concern about the status of the Bank's review of conditionality. The following is from that letter:

> The economic conditions mandated by the current debt relief and aid programs have not been shown to increase per capita income growth or reduce poverty in impoverished countries. Other examples of these economic conditions include harmful budgetary spending restrictions that undermine essential government services and the elimination of necessary assistance for small-scale agriculture and domestic manufacturing. We thus call for the World Bank to stop attaching economic policy conditions to aid and debt relief. The right of developing countries to determine their own economic future must be respected.[15]

The United Nations Children's Fund reports that humankind has never had a better chance to end severe poverty than now.

> Global prosperity is at an unprecedented level. Yet the promise to give every child a good start in life remains unfulfilled. More than half a billion children — representing a staggering 40 percent of all children in developing countries — are currently struggling to survive on less than one dollar a day. Poverty is the main cause of millions of preventable child deaths each year; it also causes tens of millions of children to go hungry, miss school or be exploited in hazardous child labor.
>
> The worst manifestations of poverty can be eradicated in less than a generation. The knowledge and techniques needed to achieve this goal already exist. Through the investment of a very modest share of the world's annual

income, all children could achieve a minimum standard of living, including access to adequate food, safe water and sanitation, primary health care and basic education. *The investment needed is estimated at $80 billion per year — less than one-third of one percent of global income* [emphasis added]. Seldom has the international community had an investment opportunity so noble in its objective and so productive in its potential.[16]

The essential cause of the horrendous suffering in the world is extreme poverty. Poverty results when currency is devalued and prices go up, when jobs are lost due to privatization, when illness strikes a mother or father and health care is not available, when children are taken out of school to work. The root cause of poverty is the injustice in the global economic system, which has provided much for the rich at the expense of the poor. The essential cause is that we who have much, much more than we need to survive, are failing to care for the poorest among us.

Chapter 5

Do the World Bank and IMF Help or Hinder?

After seven decades of trying and failing to resolve the dilemma of widespread deprivation, it's fair to wonder if the World Bank and International Monetary Fund are only doing their real jobs too well — that is, to watch out for the best interests of the world's well-off, maintain good economic global order, and make a convincing feint at actually doing something about the unspeakable misery of the majority of the planet's people.[1]

—Kevin Clarke, Senior Editor, *U.S. Catholic*

World Bank and IMF

The policies of the international financial institutions affect the livelihood of more than 4 billion people in more than 150 LDCs. The policies have worked well for some. They have not worked well for many workers in the developed countries who have lost their jobs, nor for most poor people in the LDCs. There are winners and losers. In the global economy, the rising tide has not lifted all boats.

Some experts have found that the policies of the international financial institutions have not provided economic security and stability for most people. A chief economist and senior vice president of the World Bank from 1997 to 2000 has seen firsthand the devastating effects that globalization has on developing countries, especially the poor. Joseph E. Stiglitz, winner of the Nobel Prize in economics, served on the Council of Economic Advisers under President Clinton. In 2003, he concluded:

> IMF's structural adjustment policies — the policy designed to help a country adjust to crisis as well as to more persistent imbalances — led to hunger and riots in many countries; and even when results were not so dire, even when they managed to eke out some growth for a while, often the benefits went disproportionately to the better off, with those at the bottom facing even greater poverty. What astounded me, however, was that those policies were not questioned by many of the people in power in the IMF, by those who were making the critical decisions. They were often questioned by the people in the developing countries, but many were so afraid they might lose IMF funding, and with it funding from others, that they articulated their doubts most cautiously, if at all, and only in private. But while no one was happy about the suffering that often accompanied the IMF programs, inside the IMF, it was simply assumed that whatever suffering occurred was a necessary part of the pain countries had to experience on the way to becoming a successful market economy and that their measures would, in fact, reduce the pain the countries would have to face in the long run.... The level of pain...has been far greater than necessary.[2]

Stiglitz has also written:

> A half a century after its founding, it is clear that the IMF has failed in its mission. It has not done what it is supposed to do — provide funds for countries facing an economic downturn, to enable the country to restore itself to close to

full employment. . . . IMF funds and programs not only fail to stabilize situations, in many cases they actually made the matters worse — especially for the poor.[3] . . . There is little disputing three facts: there has been little progress eliminating poverty; most of the progress has been in Asia, and especially China; and in much of the rest of the world the plight of the poor has worsened.[4]

The debt burden of the LDCs has increased steadily since the early 1980s, despite various rescheduling, restructuring, and debt conversion schemes put forward by the creditors. In 1970, the debt was $62 billion. In the late 1970s, it was $780 billion. In 1998, the total debt stood at close to $2 trillion, that is thirty-two times the amount in 1970.[5] According to the World Bank, it has continued to climb as shown in the chart on the following page.

Jean-Bertrand Aristide comments, "In the past eighteen years, we in the developing world have paid $368 billion [to the international institutions], an amount greater than what was lent to us. Why is it not possible to find the mere $80 billion that the United Nations estimates is needed to eliminate poverty on earth?"[6]

Michel Chossudovsky, author of *Globalization of Poverty in the New World Order,* quotes the words of a senior IMF official, Mohsin Khan, with regard to the efficacy of IMF programs:

Although there have been a number of studies on the subject over the past decade, one cannot say with certainty whether the programs have "worked" or not. On the basis of existing studies, one certainly cannot say whether the adoption of programs supported by the Fund led to an improvement in inflation and growth of performance. In fact, it is often found that programs are associated with a rise in inflation and a fall in the growth rate.[7]

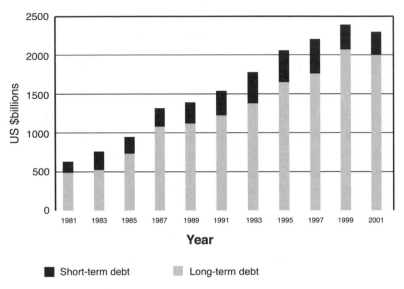

Growth in Developing Countries' External Debt

Source: Adapted from World Bank, World Debt Tables, Several Issues, Washington D.C.

Mohsin Khan has also been quoted in IMF Staff Papers:

> The social implication of these reforms (including their impact on health, education, social rights of women and the environment) have been well documented. Educational institutions are breaking down, teachers are laid off; in the health sector, there is a general breakdown in curative and preventative care as a result of the lack of medical equipment and supplies, poor working conditions and low pay of medical personnel.[8]

Other authorities have also commented on the question of whether or not poverty is being reduced. On January 28, 2000, James Wolfensohn, the president of the World Bank, was reported in the *International Herald Tribune* to have said:

"Despite years of relative peace and prosperity in industrialized countries, global poverty is getting worse. Some 1.2 billion now live in extreme poverty. More troubling still is the massive and widening gap between rich and poor."[9] The UN also reported on the question of inequality between poor and rich nations in *The Inequality Predicament: Report on the World Social Situation 2005*, finding that the inequality between poor and rich nations has deepened with the implementation of structural adjustment policies in the 1980s and the 1990s.[10] The UN reported that 80 percent of the world's gross domestic product belongs to 1 billion people living in the developed world; the remaining 20 percent is shared by 5 billion people living in the developing countries.[11]

James Galbraith, author of *A Perfect Crime: Global Inequality*, comments on the growing gap between rich and poor:

> When the global trend is isolated, we find that in the last two decades, inequality has increased throughout the world in a pattern that cuts across the effect of national income changes. During the decades that happen to coincide with the rise of neo-liberal ideology, with the breakdown of national sovereignties, and with the end of Keynesian policy in the global debt crisis of the early 1980s, *inequality rose worldwide* [emphasis added].[12]

World Trade Organization

Unlike the WB and the IMF, the WTO makes no claim to be trying to reduce poverty. It sets the rules for globalization, that is, to facilitate the transfer of goods and food. It does nothing in any country to strengthen the social net to protect those harmed by globalization. We saw in chapter 2 that workers in the LDCs who work for the outsourcing companies used by multinational corporations often do not do very well. Likewise, millions of workers in the developed countries have lost jobs due to outsourcing. Not only have millions of jobs been lost in manufacturing, but more recently the developed countries are losing more and more service-related jobs, for example, legal researchers, telemarketers, data processors, accountants, computer programmers, engineers, architects, radiologists, and scientific researchers. In the 1960s, students in Economics 101 seriously debated whether or not "what is good for GM is good for America." There is no debate today. The multinational corporations do not have a stake in providing jobs with wages that enable their workers to buy their products. The products and services provided to the developed countries come from workers on other continents. In a fiercely competitive economy, the cheaper the cost of labor the better. The corporations look for the most desperate workers. The system works as intended.

But is it working to raise the standard of living of workers? NAFTA, the first of the regional trade agreements, was signed in 1994 just before the formation of the World Trade Organization. Republicans and Democrats alike assured voters that it would create jobs, raise the standard of living in the three participating countries (Canada, the United States, and Mexico), and would stop migration. After ten years the results have been examined.

Ralph Nader's nonprofit consumer advocacy group, Public Citizen, has researched the impact of NAFTA from 1994 to 2004. Public Citizen has found that unauthorized migration from Mexico to the United States doubled from 1990 to 2000.[13] Public Citizen has uncovered many other negative economic effects of NAFTA, including:

- Over 1.5 million campesinos lost their livelihood from small farms as a result of U.S.-subsidized corn being dumped in Mexico.

- The purchasing power of the average Mexican has dropped.

- Mexican industrial wages declined approximately 25 percent.

- The poverty rate for female-headed households has increased 50 percent.

- An estimated 28,000 small to medium-size Mexican businesses were lost due to NAFTA rules, which guarantee access for Wal-Mart and other megaretailers.

- More than 38,000 U.S. small farmers have gone out of business since the passage of NAFTA.

- The United States lost 780,000 jobs in textile and apparel manufacturing.[14]

There are winners and losers as a result of NAFTA. The elites of the global corporations in both countries have done well. Workers and their families have not.

Measuring Poverty

When considering the extent of poverty described by the World Bank, it is important to consider its definition of poverty. The World Bank arbitrarily sets the poverty line at one dollar a day — or an annual income of $370 a year. So people who earn a dollar and ten cents a day, according to the World Bank, would be identified as "nonpoor." According to the World Bank definition, only 19 percent of the world's population is classified as "poor."

Recent evidence confirms that retail prices of essential consumer goods in poor countries are not appreciably lower than in the United States or Western Europe. In fact, with deregulation and "free trade," the cost of living in many Third World cities is now higher than in the United States.[15] My experience in Latin America and Haiti is that the prices of meat, fish, and fresh vegetables are about the same as in the United States. Can you imagine eating on less than one dollar a day? Can you imagine someone telling you that you are "nonpoor" because you have a dollar and ten cents a day to live on — for food, clothing, and shelter?

Surveys of household budgets for several Latin American countries suggest that at least 68 percent of the population does not meet minimum calorie and protein requirements. In Peru, for instance, after IMF reforms 83 percent of the population was unable to meet the minimum requirements. In sub-Saharan Africa and South Asia, likewise, a majority of the population suffers from chronic undernourishment.[16]

The United Nations Development Program (UNDP) also has a very biased perspective on poverty. It has devised a "human poverty index" (HPI), based on life span, access to education, and access to public and private resources. According to the HPI for Colombia, Mexico, and Thailand, only 10 or 11 percent of the people are poor. In the United States, 13 percent of the total population and 19.6 percent of the population in large cities were considered below the poverty threshold.[17]

Following this reasoning, according to UNDP estimates, the poverty levels in the United States and Germany (13.7 and 13.0 percent) are higher than poverty levels in Colombia, Mexico, and Thailand. The poverty rate in Great Britain (20 percent) is greater than the poverty rate in Zimbabwe (17.3 percent). It is clear that something is wrong with the way poverty is measured.[18]

The UNDP poverty report points to a decline of one-third to one-half in child mortality in sub-Saharan Africa, where poverty has, in fact, increased and public health programs have collapsed. What the report fails to mention is that the closing down of health clinics and the massive layoffs of health professionals — that is, those responsible for compiling mortality data — resulted in a de facto decline of *recorded* mortality, a breakdown of reliable data systems on mortality and morbidity. The poverty indicators seriously misrepresent country-level situations, as well as the seriousness of global poverty. They serve the purpose of portraying the poor as a minority group representing some 20 percent of the world population.

If a representative of the World Bank was given, say, five dollars a day to live in a Third World country, that is, 500 percent above the World Bank's poverty line, he or she would probably recognize the difficulty posed by the World Bank's definition of poverty.

Chapter 6

Keeping Unfair Structures in Place

I spent most of my time being a high-class muscle man for Big Business, for Wall Street and for the bankers. In short, I was a racketeer, a gangster for capitalism. . . . Like all members of the military profession, I never had an original thought until I left the service. My mental faculties remained in suspended animation while I obeyed the orders of the higher ups. Thus I helped make Mexico and especially Tampico safe for American oil interests in 1914. I helped make Haiti and Cuba a decent place for the National City Bank boys to collect revenues in. I helped in the raping of a half a dozen Central American Republics for the benefit of Wall Street.

— Marine Corps General Smedley Butler
as quoted in *Disturbing the Peace* [1]

The implementation of the structural adjustment policies of the 1980s and 1990s sometimes led to violent protests. Order was then maintained by military repression. Popular uprisings were brutally repressed.[2] For example:

♦ In 1989 in Caracas, the people protested when the price of bread increased 200 percent. Men, women, and children were fired upon indiscriminately. Two hundred bodies were reported to be in the Caracas morgue in the first three days of the protest. Unofficially, more than a thousand people were killed.

◆ In 1984 in Tunisia, there were bread riots by unemployed youth protesting the rise in food prices.

◆ In 1984 after the Dominican Republic complied with the demands of the international financial institutions to double prices of milk, rice, cooking oil, and medicine, riots broke out in thirty towns. After four days of riots, 112 civilians were dead and 500 wounded.[3]

◆ In 1989 in Nigeria, anti-SAP student riots resulted in the closing of six universities by the Armed Forces Ruling Council.

◆ In 1990 in Morocco, there was a general strike and popular uprising against the government IMF-sponsored reform.

◆ In 1994 in Mexico, in response to NAFTA there were insurrections led by the Zapatista Liberation Army in the Chiapas region.

In the 1970s, before the implementation of the structural adjustment policies, revolutions to change the structures of oppression were underway in Central America and some countries of South America. In Nicaragua, a bloody revolution overthrew Somoza, one of the worst dictators in Latin America. Revolutions or civil wars began in El Salvador and Guatemala, with unrest in Honduras and Panama as well.

To prevent revolutions in Central America, the U.S. government provided millions of dollars to support their militaries. The United States also trained military leaders in various techniques to suppress opposition to government policy. This was done at the School of the Americas.

The School of the Americas

The School of the Americas (SOA) originated at Fort Amador in the Panama Canal Zone in 1946 and was known as the Latin American Training Center — Ground Division. Four years later, it was renamed the U.S. Army Caribbean School. In 1963, it was again renamed as the U.S. Army School of the Americas, and in 1985 it moved to Fort Benning in Columbus, Georgia. In 2001, it was renamed the Western Hemisphere Institute for Security Cooperation.

The SOA, now located at Fort Benning, has trained more than fifty-five thousand commissioned officers, cadets, noncommissioned officers, and government civilians from twenty-two Latin American countries. Many of its graduates were responsible for ordering or participating in assassinations, torture, and

Coy/Maryknoll

Demonstration against the School of the Americas, Fort Benning, Georgia.

massacres. For many years Father Roy Bourgeois, a Maryknoll priest, has been teaching, protesting, and organizing to bring attention to and force the closing of the School of the Americas. Bourgeois was a decorated naval officer who gradually came to understand the way the military in Latin America is used to support U.S. economic interests. After serving in the navy, he became a Maryknoll priest and worked in Bolivia, where he learned firsthand how the military oppress the poor who demand justice. His life and work as founder of the School of the Americas Watch is presented in a book written by James Hodge and Linda Cooper entitled *Disturbing the Peace*.

Vicky Imerman was very helpful to the School of the Americas Watch in researching army documents to substantiate the extent of oppression and violence inflicted by SOA graduates. She is a veteran who became disillusioned with the army just as Bourgeois did with the navy. She volunteered to run the School of the Americas Watch office in Columbus, and to research army documents in the library at Fort Benning. She found that forty-six of the sixty-six officers cited for major atrocities in Latin America were trained in the School of the Americas. Among the atrocities inflicted by SOA graduates and reported in *Disturbing the Peace* are the following:

♦ Two of the three men responsible for Archbishop Romero's murder in El Salvador were trained at the School of the Americas. Two days after Archbishop Romero's assassination, the U.S. administration pushed through a multi-million-dollar aid program to El Salvador. Two months later, the Salvadoran Army massacred six hundred defenseless peasants at the Sumpul River. Most were women and children, many of whom were hacked to death and fed to dogs. Colonel Ricardo Peña Arbaiza, trained at the School of the Americas, was cited for this massacre.

- Three of the five cited for the rape and murder of U.S. missionaries in El Salvador (Ita Ford, Dorothy Kazel, Maura Clark, and Jean Donovan) were trained at the School of the Americas. One of the three was General Carlos Vides Casanova, the former defense minister of El Salvador, who was a guest speaker at the School of the Americas five years after the murders.

- Ten of the twelve officers who oversaw the El Mozote massacre were trained at the School of the Americas. At El Mozote, U.S.-trained Salvadoran troops shot, hanged, and decapitated more than nine hundred peasants, mostly women and elderly villagers.

- Nineteen of the twenty-six cited in the assassination of five Jesuit priests, their cook, and her daughter in El Salvador were trained at the School of the Americas. U.S. Army Major Eric Bucklan reported that he was told that Colonel Guillermo Alfredo Benavides helped plan the murders. Bucklan, a U.S. military advisor, had knowledge of the scheme well in advance of the assassinations.

- General Hector Gramajo, an SOA graduate, was defense minister in El Salvador when Sister Dianna Ortiz was kidnapped. She had been teaching Mayan children to read and write. She was taken to a clandestine prison where she was gang raped, burned more than a hundred times with cigarettes, and lowered into a pit with the bodies of "children, women, and men, some decapitated, some lying face up and caked with blood, some dead, some alive — and all swarming with rats." In 1995, U.S. District Judge Douglas Woodlock found that Gramajo was aware of and supported widespread acts of brutality committed by personnel under his command, resulting in thousands of civilian deaths.

- In Honduras two Catholic priests, Michael Jerome Cypher and Ivan Bentancur, were castrated and had their eyes gouged out. They were thrown into a well with two women and the bodies of five peasants who had been roasted alive in bread ovens. Arrested in the case were SOA graduates Major José Enrique Chinchilla and Lieutenant Benjamin Plota.

- John Negroponte, the U.S. ambassador to Honduras who oversaw the early years of the Contra operation in Nicaragua, pressured the Honduran president Roberto Suazo to make General Gustavo Alvarez Martínez the head of the Honduran armed forces. Alvarez created Battalion 3-16, a death squad that contracted Contras as hit men. Alvarez was trained at the School of the Americas. Contra commanders were former national guardsmen, almost all of whom Somoza had sent through the School of the Americas.

- Father James "Guadalupe" Carney, a Jesuit missionary in El Salvador, was tortured and thrown out of a helicopter on orders of General Gustavo Alvarez Martínez, the same year Reagan gave the general the Legion of Merit Award.

- The 2000 Human Rights Watch Report, *The Ties That Bind,* documented the Colombian military's ties to violent paramilitary groups and drug traffickers — and linked at least seven SOA graduates to human rights abuses.

- Guatemalan Bishop Juan José Gerardi released a report entitled *Guatemala: Nunca Mas* (Never Again), which implicated the Guatemalan army and its paramilitaries in almost 90 percent of the atrocities committed in Guatemala. SOA graduates figure prominently among the officers cited for abuse. Two days after releasing the report, the bishop was assassinated.

- On January 17, 2001, the day the Western Hemisphere Institute for Security Cooperation (formerly known as the School of the Americas) reopened, right-wing Colombian paramilitaries dragged twenty-five people from their homes during the night and crushed their skulls with sledgehammers and rocks. The sledgehammer massacre was only one of twenty-six atrocities in Colombia that month. More than twenty-five thousand Colombians died violently the year before, and some 2 million had been terrorized into fleeing their homes.

- Hundreds of peasants in Colombia were killed and dismembered in the Trujillo Chainsaw Massacre. The executions were carried out by SOA graduate Major Alirio Antonio Urueña Jaramillo. The crimes were reported by an army informant, Daniel Arcila. In his report, Arcila said the victims were tortured before being killed. Their fingernails were pried off, their feet were cut, salt was poured into their wounds, they were burned with a blow torch on different parts of their body, and their skin was peeled off. The men were emasculated and their penises and testicles put in their mouths. Finally, they were quartered with a chainsaw.

- More than three thousand political opponents of Augusto Pinochet in Chile were kidnapped, tortured, and executed. Most of Pinochet's security forces were trained at the School of the Americas.

Training Manuals for Repression

SOA training manuals used from 1982 to 1991 advocated torture and execution, but this was not new. Alfred McCoy, professor of history at the University of Wisconsin–Madison and author of *Closer Than Brothers: A Study on the Impact of the CIA Torture Methods,* has studied torture techniques used by the CIA over the last fifty years. Throughout the 1950s and early 1960s, the CIA financed and conducted secret research on coercion and human consciousness. McCoy said, "The scale of that research should not be minimized. By the late 1950s, it reached a billion dollars a year. The agency was providing the majority of the funding for half a dozen leading psychology departments."[4] In an article entitled "Roots of Abu Ghraib in CIA Techniques" James Hodge and Linda Cooper report how torture has been taught and implemented by the CIA from the 1950s to the present. [5] The basic torture techniques that resulted from the research departments involved the use of stress positions, sensory deprivation, and sexual humiliation. In 1963, the techniques were codified in a secret manual known as the *KUBARK Counterintelligence Interrogation*. By 1967, the CIA operated some forty interrogation centers in Vietnam as part of its Phoenix program. The KUBARK manual served as a model for the CIA's *Human Resource Exploitation Training Manual* used in the 1980s in Honduras. Florencio Caballero, a CIA-trained interrogator in Honduras, said in a *New York Times* article entitled "Testifying to Torture" (June 5, 1988) that he and others were taught "to study the fears and weaknesses of the prisoner. To make him stand up, don't let him sleep, keep him naked and in isolation, put rats and cockroaches in his cell, give him bad food, serve him dead animals, throw water on him, change the temperature."

Six manuals of torture were used at the School of the Americas from 1982 to 1991. They advocated execution of guerrillas, extortion, physical abuse, and coercion. They were kept secret until 1996, when they were disclosed by the Pentagon, which feared that Congressman Joseph Kennedy had a copy of the manuals. Kennedy conducted a five-year campaign to close the school. In *Disturbing the Peace* he is reported as saying: "According to the Pentagon's own excerpts, School of the Americas' students were advised to imprison those from whom they were seeking information, to 'involuntarily' obtain information from those sources — in other words, torture them; to arrest their parents; to use 'motivation by fear,' pay bounties for enemy dead; execute opponents; subvert the press; and use torture, blackmail, and even injections of truth serum to obtain information."[6]

The torture techniques used in Iraq are the same as those used for decades and codified in manuals, that is, the use of stress positions, sensory deprivation, and sexual humiliation. The long-term systematic use of these torture techniques is documented in two recent books, *Truth, Torture, and the American Way* by Jennifer Harbury and *Torture: Religious Ethics and National Security* by John Perry. The media have reported extensively on the scandal of the torture inflicted by soldiers and by others on behalf of the CIA. But I have never read or heard in the major media any commentary that connects the dots to conclude that the torture policy of the United States was systematic and long term. There is no question, however, that there has been long-term systematic use of torture and military force, both open and clandestine, to maintain the status quo and the flow of food, goods, and resources from the south to the north in the Americas.

Chapter 7

The Uses of Slaves
in the Global Economy

Kevin Bales, author of *Disposable People: New Slavery in the Global Economy,* concludes that there are more slaves alive today than all of the slaves captured in Africa from the sixteenth through the nineteenth centuries. Estimates range from 27 million to as high as 200 million.[1]

Although we might not be aware of it, slavery supports the lifestyle of many people in developed countries. Slaves work as maids in households in Washington, DC, Paris, London, New York, Zurich, and other major cities. Slaves in Pakistan may have made your shoes. In India, they may have made your carpet. Slaves may have cut and sewn your clothing in Bangladesh. The sugar on your table may have come from slave labor in the Caribbean. In Burma, tens of thousands of men, women, and children are used as laborers or bearers in military campaigns against indigenous people or on construction sites. In the United States, farm workers have been found working under armed guards as field slaves. Slaves may have made bricks for the factory that made your TV. They may have grown the rice that fed the woman who wove the cloth of your curtains. Slaves are used to make jewelry. They work in mines. They make fireworks. They clear forests to make charcoal that is used in steel mills to make metal components used in cars. In Brazil, slaves harvest sugar. They mine gold and precious stones. They work as prostitutes.

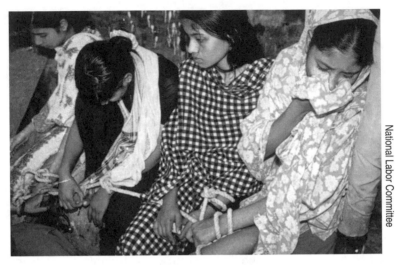

National Labor Committee

Garment workers in Bangladesh roped together.

The rubber industry relies on slavery. So do producers of cattle and timber.

It is hard to imagine the horrors experienced by women and children who have been sold to become sex slaves. In an article entitled "Stopping Traffic" Maryknoll Sister Helene O'Sullivan points out that " ... in the last thirty years, traffic of women and children in Asia for sexual exploitation has victimized more than 30 million people. The CIA estimates that fifty thousand people are trafficked into the United States each year. . . . Girls as young as thirteen, mostly from Asia and Eastern Europe, are trafficked as 'mail order brides.' "[2]

Enslaved Thai and Filipino women have been freed from incredibly lucrative brothels in New York, Seattle, and Los Angeles. Bales reports that a girl who costs $150 can be sold for sex up to ten times a night to bring in $10,000 a month. Bales reports that a girl between twelve and fifteen years old can be purchased for $800 to $2,000, and the cost of running a brothel and feeding the girls is relatively low. The profit is often as high as 800 percent a year. This kind of return can be made on a girl for five to ten years. After that, especially if she has become ill or HIV-positive, the girl is dumped.[3]

The International Organization for Migration estimates that twenty thousand women are trafficked annually from southeastern Asia, including women from the region and women brought there for the sex trade.[4] In 1986, it was estimated that there were twenty thousand children in the Philippines involved in the sex trade; in 2000, the estimate rose to a hundred thousand.[5] According to a survey by *India Today Magazine,* there are between four hundred thousand and five hundred thousand child prostitutes in India.[6] In Mexico, a study of six cities (Acapulco, Cancún, Cuidad Juárez, Guadalajara, Tapachula, and Tijuana) estimates that a total of forty-six hundred children are sexually exploited. At the national level, some sixteen thousand children are believed to be exploited.[7]

Pamela Shifman and Ken Franzblau of Equality Now, an international human rights organization that advocates the rights of girls and women around the world, reported on the trafficking of girls and women in the United States.

> In the United States, the Federal Bureau of Investigation raided a house in Atlanta, Georgia, after acquiring information that its occupants were engaged in a large-scale prostitution operation that recruited teenage Vietnamese girls. Ultimately, thirteen individuals were charged under a number of different laws with smuggling, imprisoning and forcing into prostitution almost a thousand women and girls, some as young as thirteen. The women and girls from China, the Lao People's Democratic Republic, Malaysia, Thailand and Vietnam were smuggled into the United States for fees ranging from $30,000 to $40,000,

which they were forced to pay back by working as prostitutes.... The women and girls were not able to leave the premises unless they were escorted by their captors. Armed Vietnamese gang members were used as guards and enforcers. The women and girls were moved across the United States every week to ten days to service men in thirteen different states.

The United States Central Intelligence Agency estimates that some 45,000 to 50,000 women and children are trafficked annually to the United States, bound for the sex industry or for factory or other work under egregious labor conditions.... Trafficking through Mexico to the United States is one of the most prevalent routes.[8]

At the bus stations in Thailand, gangs watch for women or children who can be snatched or drugged for shipment to brothels. At the Port Authority Bus Terminal in New York City, predators also are on the lookout for newly arrived teenagers who may be runaways. They befriend the children with the hope of becoming their pimp.

The price of your car and the prices of metal products in your home may have been "subsidized" by the labor of slaves. Kevin Hall reports that U.S. companies imported virtually all of the 2.2 million tons of pig iron that northern Brazil produced in 2004.[9] One of the biggest buyers was the Nucor Corporation of Charlotte, North Carolina. Nucor buys pig iron from Ferro Jusa do Maranhão, a Brazilian pig iron maker. Labor inspectors determined that Ferro Jusa do Maranhão was buying charcoal from a ranch that used slave labor.

Kevin Bales has reported on the hazards faced by the slaves who make the charcoal used to make steel in Brazil. The charcoal workers are "temporary slaves." After a few months, they are too sick to continue to work. These young men are left permanently disabled by black lung disease. They must work in small ovens, or *batterias,* which are about seven feet high and ten feet wide. They enter the oven through an opening about four feet high. They stack wood very tightly, seal the door with brick and mud, and then set the fire. The wood slowly burns to charcoal during two days and then the workers have to enter to get the charcoal out. Every bit of fat was burnt off all the workers seen by Bales. The workers breathe enormous quantities of black dust. They cough and spit constantly. It is extremely hot. They have to stand on piles of charcoal. If they trip they fall onto red hot coals. All the charcoal workers had burn scars on their hands, arms, and legs. Many had open cuts, still swollen and festering. Armed guards prevent the men from leaving the camps where they work.

Hall found that processed and cooked meats, soybeans, and other produce that we import were produced on farms cleared by slaves. We import hardwoods such as *cumara, ipe,* and *jatoba,* which are harvested or made accessible to loggers by slaves. They are sold in Home Depot as Brazilian cherry, Brazilian teak, and Brazilian walnut. In January 2004, three Ministry of Labor inspectors and their driver were killed near Brasilia while investigating slavery.

Adilson Prestes, a Brazilian human rights activist, denounced a chain of illegal activities including slavery. He stood up to landowners in the town of Novo Progresso and was shot to death on July 3, 2003, in front of his home. Marcelo Campos, head of the Anti-Slavery Program at the Brazilian Ministry of Labor, stated: "Legal slaves were property and watched over because they were an asset. They had food and shelter because the owner needed to make sure they stayed alive. Today's slave is not a concern. The landowner uses them as an absolutely temporary item, like a disposable razor."

Tarcisio Feitosa, head of the Altamira office of the Pastoral Land Commission, the Roman Catholic Church's rural social work arm, said: "In Rio de Janeiro or São Paulo or Santa Catarina, we live in a democracy, but here in the Amazon it doesn't exist. Tomorrow I can wake up and somebody can shoot me in my home. Here, the state does not offer protection."[10]

Whether we realize it or not, whether we want it or not, the lifestyle of many people in the developed countries is supported by slave labor. Poor people subsidize rich people, who purchase food and consumer goods produced at starvation wages. And sometimes poor people subsidize the rich with their very lives.

Chapter 8

The Politics of Food

The reason so many people are dying of hunger is not because there isn't enough food. Virtually every "hungry" country produces enough food for all of its people. The essential problem is that food is not distributed fairly. Distribution is regulated by political and economic decision makers, and rarely by the people themselves. It is the powerful who decide who has access to an abundant food supply and who does not. In the last twenty-five years, there have been significant improvements in food production, yet the problem of world hunger is growing.

In 1981, the problem was described by a group of Nobel Prize Laureates in their *Manifesto against Hunger and Under-development.*

We are men and women of science and literature dedicated to peace. Our religious, historical and cultural backgrounds vary, but we have all been honored for seeking and celebrating what is true in life, what is alive in truth; and our work expresses our search for universal understanding, for brotherhood and the shared civilization that is found in peace and progress. We appeal to all men and women of good will, those in power, and to all ordinary people, whatever their responsibilities may be, to bring back to life the millions who, as victims of political and economic upheavals of the world today, are suffering from hunger and privation.... Their situation has no precedent.

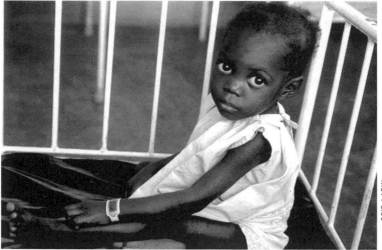

A Haitian child.

In a single year, more people suffer than all those who
have died in the holocaust of the first half of this century.
Every day spreads the outrage further, an outrage that as-
saults both the world around us and our own spirit and
consciousness. . . . Everyone who denounces this tragic state
of affairs and seeks to remedy it knows its causes are primarily political. . . . We must refute the false idea of reality
that accepts as inevitable what is in fact a result of present
politics; in other words, of organized chaos. . . . We cannot
be so irresponsible as to watch the disaster that threatens
us and do nothing about it. We know that the entire human
race is in danger, and we must use this knowledge to create
hope and salvation, to give substance to what we believe
in, what we hope for. . . . If the news media and those who
have honored us will only listen to what we are saying;
if they will only take notice of what we are doing and
what many others with the same ideas are doing; if only

people were told what is happening, then the world's dark future, which now seeks to threaten everyone in it, may be changed. . . . But only if we take action. Now is the time to act, now is the time to create, now is the time to live in a way that will give life to others.[1]

On June 28, 1987, in an article in the *New York Times* entitled "World Hunger Still Found Growing," Paul Lewis cited UN conclusions that the number of hungry and malnourished people has been increasing at a quickening pace while the world was awash with cheap surplus food. The UN found record harvests in many places of the world while the estimated number of hungry people grew from 340 million in 1980 to 720 million in 1986.

In 2005, Bread for the World reported that the number of people who suffered worldwide from hunger and malnutrition in the year 2003 was 852 million.[2]

Food Myths

Food First, also known as the Institute for Food and Development Policy, is a nonprofit research and education center based in San Francisco and dedicated to investigating and exposing the root causes of hunger. The institute describes the myths that prevent us from understanding the causes of hunger.[3] Among the myths are the following:

Myth 1: There simply isn't enough food to go around.

There is enough wheat, rice, and other grains produced to feed every person with 3,600 calories a day — much more than we need. The reality is that many poor countries export more food than they import. India is one example. India is actually the top food exporter in the developing world.

Myth 2: Nature is to blame.

We often think of the natural disasters of famine and flood as responsible for starvation in poor countries. Since 1960, the number of natural disasters has not increased, yet death due to natural disasters has increased sixfold. People are more vulnerable to national disasters, and more people live on the brink of disaster because they have been deprived of land by the powerful few, or they are trapped by the unremitting grip of debt, heavy taxation, and starvation wages. Most deaths from famines or floods result from unjust economic and political arrangements — not from acts of God. What we call natural disasters are actually social or political disasters.

Myth 3: There are too many mouths to feed; hunger is caused by overpopulation.

Although rapid population growth is a serious concern in many countries, nowhere does population density explain hunger. Like hunger itself, it results from underlying inequities that deprive people, especially poor women, of economic opportunities. People without land and resources rely on the labor power of their families. Where malnutrition takes the lives of many children, high birth rates help ensure that some will survive, thereby enhancing the survival chances of the family. Children as young as six provide economic benefit to the family; by age twelve they contribute more than they consume. With more children there is greater economic security for the family.

Myth 4: The green revolution is the answer.

The green revolution's production advances over the past three decades is no myth. With higher yields resulting from chemical fertilizers, irrigation, and pesticides, the "miracle" seeds help produce 50 million additional tons of wheat and rice a year. But a narrow focus on boosting production can never help the hungry because it fails to improve — and may even worsen — the distribution of economic power that determines who can afford to eat. In the very countries most touted as green revolution success stories — India, Indonesia, Mexico, and the Philippines — production of the green revolution grains has increased while hunger has worsened. An Indian farm worker once reminded us, "If you don't own the land, you never get enough to eat, no matter how much it is producing." Hunger can be alleviated only by redistributing food-producing resources and purchasing power to the hungry.

The Impact of Agricultural Subsidies on Hunger

Governments of the developed countries give subsidies to their farmers, who then can sell their crops at prices lower than the market price. This is very beneficial to the farmers in the developed countries, but extremely harmful to farmers in poor countries. This means farmers in poor countries are not able to export their crops and have to lower their prices when sold in-country. This is a serious problem because in poor countries the largest workforce is in agriculture.

There is a bitter irony. Subsidies drive down the prices of food, which is good for consumers, but they also destroy local agriculture, the most important industry in poor countries. Jean-Bertrand Aristide, president of Haiti, reported on the problem of rice subsidies in the United States.

What happens to poor countries when they embrace free trade? In Haiti in 1986 we imported just 7,000 tons of rice, the main staple food for the country. The vast majority was grown in Haiti. In the late 1980s, Haiti complied with free trade policies advocated by the international lending agencies and lifted tariffs on rice imports. Cheaper rice immediately flooded in from the United States, where the rice industry is subsidized. In fact, the liberalization of Haiti's market coincided with the 1985 Farm Bill in the United States, which increased subsidies to the rice industry so that 40 percent of U.S. rice growers' profit came from the government by 1987. Haiti's peasant farmers could not possibly compete. By 1996 Haiti was importing 196,000 tons of rice at a cost of $100 million a year. Haitian rice production became negligible. Once dependence on foreign rice was complete, import prices began to rise, leaving Haiti's population, particularly the urban poor, completely at the whim of rising world grain prices. And the prices continue to rise.... A hungry nation became hungrier.[4]

Two priests, Fathers Cesar Ferrari and Carlos Novoa, S.J., comment on the effect of agricultural subsidies in *America*, the magazine of the Jesuits:

International organizations like the International Monetary Fund and the World Bank are not much help. These "champions" of free trade have no influence on the economic policies of developed countries, which are violating free trade principles with their agricultural subsidies.... When the IMF and World Bank press developing countries to reduce their fiscal deficits as a condition of aid, the governments cannot use agricultural subsidies to offset the subsidies of developed countries.... Justice and economic principles of free trade demand a progressive reduction of agricultural subsidies to growers in developed countries and the tariffs that wealthy people impose on imports from poor countries.... Resistance by wealthy nations to the reduction of these subsidies and tariffs is leading to the suffering and deaths of millions of people. A recent study by the World Health Organization notes that six million children die of hunger around the world every year.[5]

The average person in sub-Saharan Africa earns less than one dollar a day. The average cow in Europe earns about two dollars a day, thanks to government subsidies. The European Union's policy has spawned subsidies and tariffs that have richly rewarded European farms and swollen European food output, while depressing world food prices and undercutting Africa's exports. Steve Chapman of the *Chicago Tribune* reported the following:

> The problem is that, as everyone knows by now, the surest remedy for poverty is trade, not aid. Countries that have learned to compete in world commerce have far outdistanced countries that are forced to rely on international handouts. But the trade policies of the United States and other industrialized nations have closed off the best escape route.
>
> Africa, with thirteen percent of the world's people, accounts for only two percent of global trade. Why? One reason is that it has been deprived of access to the most lucrative customers. As the international aid group Oxfam pointed out last year: "When developing countries export to rich country markets, they face tariff barriers that are four times higher than those encountered by rich countries."...The world trading system, of which the United States makes up a huge part, is rigged against Africans. We are more intent on protecting a few American producers than on helping the vast mass of the world's poor.
>
> Cotton, for example, is a major crop in many African countries, where it can be grown much cheaper than in most places. But cotton prices have plunged in the last

decade — mainly because the United States and other countries pay our farmers to grow it. The more we subsidize cotton farmers, the more cotton there is on the world market, and the lower the price.

Our growers don't feel the pain so much because of all their federal aid; they each get an average of $50,000 a year in subsidies. But African dirt farmers, who are poor to begin with, don't enjoy such protection. They get the full brunt of the artificially low prices. American cotton subsidies cost Africa $300 million annually. And $300 million is real money to people accustomed to living on less than a dollar a day.... A study by the International Monetary Fund found that benefits to Africa were only one-fifth of what they would have been under a genuine free trade regime.[6]

An editorial in *Business Week* commented: "The United States, Europe and Japan spend $300 billion a year to subsidize farmers. These subsidies, by destroying international markets, crush the cotton growers of Pakistan, the rice farmers of Indonesia, and millions of other people throughout the Third World."[7]

Why do countries ravaged by famine export food? Why do the elite in poor nations sell vast quantities of food to rich nations while many of their own people are malnourished or starving? History provides numerous examples of private traders exporting food in the middle of famine. It happened in Ireland in the 1840s. It happened in India in the 1870s. The same thing happened recently in Africa.[8] It is happening today. The powerful in the developed countries collaborate with the elite in poor countries to perpetuate the system in which the poor feed the rich. It is the poor that plant the seeds, tend the crops, and gather the harvest sent to the rich nations.

Chapter 9

Women and Children Are Hurt the Most

The first step toward understanding injustice in our world is to realize that whether or not people are hungry, whether or not they have health care, education, and safe water depends upon decisions made by the powerful and wealthy. It is hard and at times seemingly impossible for those who are well off to recognize that they are part of an economic and political system that treats people so poorly. Instead we would like to think that poverty exists because women have too many children. Or that poor people are not so smart, that they are lazy, or that their countries lack natural resources. We would like to think that hunger results from natural disasters such as drought or from corrupt governments siphoning off needed resources.

One morning at the St. Catherine Siena Grammar School in Vineland, New Jersey, I showed slides to kindergarten children of very poor children in Latin America who live on the streets. I was trying to be very gentle with them in my effort to help them see, as Jesus did, that the children are the bearers of the kingdom — that Jesus especially loved the children.

One boy asked, "Why don't the adults do something?" He was very upset. I said that the adults care, but they are busy with their families and their jobs. He said, "No, they don't care." I was startled at his response, but I think the child was right. Despite all the exhortations in the Bible about caring for orphans

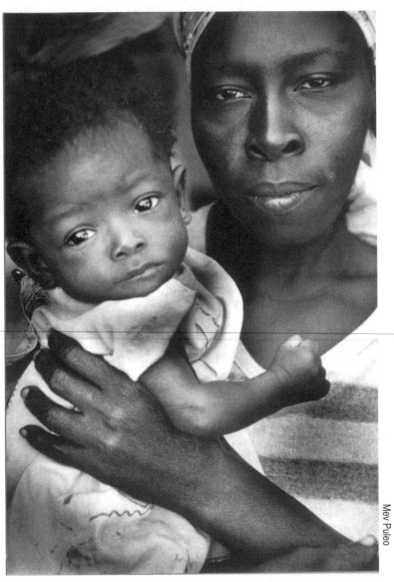

Mev Puleo

Haitian mother and child.

and widows, why don't we care enough about the suffering of women and children to do something about it? The bare facts from the developing countries show how serious and pervasive the problem really is.

Women

+ In Latin America, 71 percent of female children are underweight; 17 percent of male children are.[1]

+ In India in the State of Punjab, 21 percent of girls in low income families suffer severe malnutrition; 3 percent of the boys do.[2]

+ Nine hundred million people in the world cannot read. Two-thirds are women.[3]

+ In China, South Asia, and West Asia, there are only ninety-four women for every one hundred men. Harvard economist Amartya Sen has estimated that in Asia, there are 100 million women "missing" — 49 million in China alone. Since these societies value boys more than girls, female babies are aborted or abandoned.[4]

+ Ninety percent of the workforce in the export processing zones in Latin America are women. In many factories, women report physical abuse, sexual harassment, and violence, as well as mandatory pregnancy testing.[5]

+ Women in the export processing zones in Latin America work as many as eighty hours a week and earn fifty-six to eighty-seven cents an hour. Despite national economic growth in Mexico and El Salvador, wages have fallen for women in export processing zones.[6]

- ♦ Women in the Americas, both North and South, have seen their wages decline and their workloads double because of trade liberalization.[7]
- ♦ In the United States, men earn 25 percent more than women. In Brazil, men earn 47 percent more than women.[8]

Children

The United Nations Development Program has reported on the extent of child poverty and deprivation. Over one-half of all children are severely deprived and over one-third are living in absolute poverty.[9]

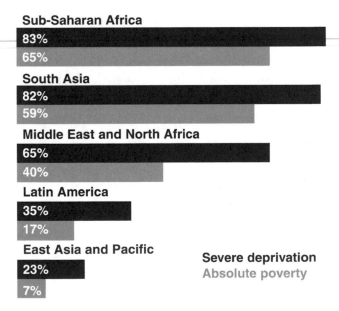

Incidence of Child Poverty
and Severe Deprivation, by Region

Sub-Saharan Africa
83%
65%

South Asia
82%
59%

Middle East and North Africa
65%
40%

Latin America
35%
17%

East Asia and Pacific
23%
7%

Severe deprivation
Absolute poverty

- Every year, 11 million children die — most under the age of five and more than 6 million from completely preventable causes.[10]

- Almost 7 million children in developing countries live in absolute poverty and over 1 billion are severely deprived.[11]

- Every year, more than 20 million low-birth-weight babies are born in developing countries. These babies risk dying in infancy, while those who survive often suffer lifelong physical and cognitive disabilities.[12]

- Every day, more than six thousand children die from hunger-related causes — one child every five seconds.[13]

- In 2003, there were an estimated 15 million AIDS orphans around the world, expected to increase to 25 million by 2010.[14]

- Some 8.4 million children work in the worst forms of child labor, including debt bondage, where children essentially endure slavery to pay off inherited family debt.[15]

- The number of prostituted children is thought to be increasing and could be as high as 10 million.[16]

Whether or not the policies of the international financial institutions over the long run are beneficial for the economies of developing countries is debated. Some argue that there would be no "long-term gain" without "short-term pain." There is no debate about whether or not women and children pay the highest price when structural adjustment programs are implemented. Cuts in government spending lead women to increase their workloads to respond to the increased price of household goods and food. It is mostly women who feed the children, care for the sick, gather and prepare the food, wash the clothes, clean the house, and carry the water. When the currency in poor countries is devalued and government services are cut, it is mostly the women who have to make up the difference to ensure that the children get what they can. And most of the work done by women is taken for granted and not given value by society. This affects their status, opportunities, and power.

To address the special needs of women, the World Bank established its "Women in Development Unit," but it was not until 1994 that the Bank endorsed its first gender policy paper, from which its Operational Policy was derived. In 1995 James Wolfensohn, the World Bank president, attended the Fourth World Conference on Women held in Beijing. Since that conference, the Bank has provided over $5 billion in lending for girls' education. It also has become the largest provider of external funds for health, population, and nutrition in low- and middle-income countries, and since the Beijing conference, over two-thirds of the Bank loans in these three areas have included gender-specific objectives. While the World Bank has provided significant support to women in many ways, the Women in Development Funding Projects are conditioned upon "satisfactory compliance" with IMF–World Bank conditionalities (structural adjustment policies), that is, devaluation, budget austerity, the application of user fees in health and education, the phasing out of state-sponsored credit trade liberalization, the deregulation of grain markets, the elimination of minimum wage legislation, and so on. In other words, donor support to women's programs — via Women in Development funded projects — is conditional upon prior degradation of women's rights.[17]

According to the biennial report of the United Nations Development Fund for Women (UNIFEM), over the past two decades the process of globalization has contributed to widening inequality within and among countries. It has been punctuated by economic and social collapse in parts of sub-Saharan Africa and countries in transition and by financial crises in Asia and Latin America. UNIFEM points out that if a wide range of people are to gain, globalization must be reshaped so that it is more people-centered instead of profit-centered and more accountable to women.[18]

The Poverty Reduction Strategy Papers of the International Monetary Fund were examined by the UK Gender and Development Network in a report authored by Anne Whitehead entitled *Failing Women, Sustaining Poverty: Gender and Poverty Reduction Strategy Papers*.[19] This report examined how the Poverty Reduction Strategy Papers (PRSPs) in four countries deal with gender issues. Whitehead found that gender issues appear in a fragmented and arbitrary way in the body of the PRSPs dealing with policy strategy and budget commitments. They pay limited attention to the women's material well-being, and there is no recognition that macroeconomic policies and national budgets can be gendered. Government efforts to listen to and consult women at all levels were unsatisfactory.

Whitehead also found that consultation with civil society organizations (CSOs) in general were flawed, and civil society representatives had to work very hard to get their views recorded. Women citizens were hardly consulted at all, and gender advocates within national CSOs had little success in influencing strategies. These views were rarely then reflected in the content of the PRSPs. Women's voices have hardly been sought and have definitely not been heard.

Violence against Women

Perhaps the most pervasive human rights violation in the world today is the physical and sexual abuse suffered by girls and women. UNIFEM reports the following:

> Violence against women is a public health emergency and a major cause of death and disability for women sixteen to

forty-four years of age. At least one in every three women around the world has been beaten, coerced into sex, or otherwise abused in her lifetime. In no country in the world are women safe from this type of violence. In 2005, UNIFEM found that more than 50 percent of the women in Bangladesh, Ethiopia, Peru and Tanzania reported having been subjected to physical or sexual violence by intimate partners, with figures reaching a staggering 71 percent in rural Ethiopia. UNIFEM reported on an earlier World Health Organization study that put the number of women physically abused by their partners or ex-partners at 30 percent in the UK and 22 percent in the United States. Based on several surveys from around the world, half of the women who die from homicides are killed by their current or former husbands or partners. They die from gun violence, beatings and burns, among numerous other forms of violence. UNIFEM reports that in the United States, 700,000 women are raped or sexually assaulted each year with 14.8 percent of the women having been raped before the age of seventeen.[20]

Female Genital Mutilation (FGM)

Female genital mutilation includes various traditional cutting operations performed on women and children. It is sometimes justified as a way to ensure chastity. FGM occurs primarily in over twenty-five African countries, among some minorities in Asia, and among immigrant communities in the United States, Europe, Australia, and Canada. An estimated 130 million today have undergone FGM and an additional 2 million girls and women are being subjected to it each year.[21]

Dowry Murders

Dowry murder is the killing of a woman by her husband or in-laws because her family is unable to pay for her dowry. There are close to fifteen thousand dowry deaths a year in southeast Asia, mostly in kitchen fires designed to look like accidents. In 2002, 315 women and girls in Bangladesh were victims of acid attacks related to a failure to pay dowries.[22]

Honor Killings

In many societies, rape victims, women suspected of engaging in premarital sex, and women accused of adultery have been murdered by their male relatives because the violation of the women's chastity is viewed as an affront to the family's honor. UNIFEM points out that more than one thousand women are killed in Pakistan in the name of honor every year. They found that in Jordan and Lebanon, 70 to 75 percent of the perpetrators were the woman's brother.[23]

Early Marriage

The practice of early marriage is prevalent throughout the world, especially in Africa and South Asia. This is a form of sexual violence, since young girls are often forced into the marriage and into sexual relations, which jeopardize their health, raise their risk of exposures to HIV/AIDS, and limit their chance of attending school. It also may result in fistulas.[24]

Fistulas

In many parts of the developing world and in Africa in particular, women face the greatest number of health problems, many of which are connected to giving birth. In many rural areas in Ethiopia, for example, girls are given to husbands just after they experience their first menstrual flow — between nine and fifteen years of age. Many become impregnated before they develop enough pelvic width to give birth. Young girls may be in labor without medical help for five or six days. Eventually the baby dies and passes. The prolonged pressure of the baby's head against the mother's pelvis cuts off the blood supply to the soft tissue surrounding her bladder, rectum, and vagina, leading to tissue necrosis. A fistula, or a hole, is the result. If the hole is created between the vagina and the bladder, she has continuous leakage of urine. If the hole is between her vagina and rectum, she loses control of her bowel movements. Most women who suffer fistulas will be unaware that medical treatment is possible and even for those who know this, treatment may not be available in their area or they may not have the money to obtain it. Some simply cannot afford transportation to the hospital.

Can you imagine the anguish of the father and mother when their daughter with the fistula is returned to them by her husband? Instead of her beginning her new life as mother and wife, she will likely be placed in a hut alongside the family house because the odor of the continually dripping urine and fecal matter will be too strong for her to live with others. She will likely be ostracized from the community and suffer depression, shame, and self-loathing. Some fistula victims turn to commercial sex or are forced to beg. Most fistulas can be repaired at a cost of between $100 and $400. This is far beyond what most poor families can afford. The World Health Organization reports that over 2 million women are currently living with obstetric fistulas. Estimates based on the number of people who seek treatment in hospitals and clinics are likely to be low because many women never seek care.[25]

Poverty is the fundamental cause of fistula. Inadequate nutrition, stunted growth, limited access to health care, and the traditions of early marriage and pregnancy contribute to the likelihood of obstructed labor. Traditional practices such as female genital cutting can also result in formation of a fistula. In Africa, there are fifty thousand to a hundred thousand new fistula patients each year. Women with untreated fistulas face slow premature death from frequent infection and kidney failure.

The medical literature shows that 80 to 90 percent of the cases can be successfully treated so the women can return to full, normal lives. Fistula repair centers operate in only a few countries, most notably Ethiopia and Nigeria, but these centers cannot meet the enormous need for fistula care. Obstetric fistula is an issue inextricably linked to the lower status accorded to women and girls. It is an issue of human rights.[26]

Mass Murder by Complacency: HIV/AIDS

The AIDS epidemic may become the greatest catastrophe to ever hit the human race. Stephen Louis, UN Special Envoy for AIDS in Africa, has called the lack of adequate response "mass murder by complacency."

◆ In 2003, 26.6 million people in sub-Saharan Africa suffered with HIV/AIDS associated illnesses.[27]

◆ Young women are 1.6 times more likely to be living with HIV than young men.[28]

◆ In the Caribbean, young women are 2.5 times more likely to be living with HIV than young men.[29]

◆ The incidence of AIDS among females fifteen to twenty-four years of age is three to six times higher than that of males in the same age group.[30]

In the United States, people with AIDS can live productive lives with the help of medicine. Few in Africa have access to medication, where eight thousand people die every day of AIDS. In some African countries, 30 percent of the population between fifteen and forty-nine years old is infected with the AIDS virus. In Zimbabwe, at one university, 68 percent of the teachers and students were HIV-positive. Prevalence rates indicate a disproportionate impact on women and girls in sub-Saharan Africa, where 77 percent of all HIV-positive women reside.[31] Very few of those infected in poor countries have access to medication. Without effective preventative programs, the impact on Asia is expected to be worse than that on Africa.

Antiretroviral drugs are essential to fighting AIDS. The World Trade Organization signed an agreement in 2003 permitting countries to import generic drugs (at about one-fifth of the cost of brand-name equivalents) without violating patent rights. The United States refused to sign it without the addition of further conditions that eligible countries must meet. The Bush administration may also restrict the trade of generic drugs through international free-trade agreements.

Françoise Héritier comments:

> We live in a time in which violence is right before our very eyes. The word is applied to extremely varied contexts, but each is marked by open violence — by violent acts, fury, hatred, massacres, cruelty, collective atrocities — but also by the cloaked violences of economic domination, of labor-capital relations, of the great north-south divide, to say nothing of all of the "everyday" violences perpetrated against the weak: women, children, all those excluded by the social system.[32]

The prices of goods made and services performed in the United States include the costs that some employers pay for health care for their workers and family members. The price we pay for products and food that we receive from the labor of the poor would be higher if workers in indebted nations had greater access to health care. In a very real sense, we get a free ride on the backs of poor workers who subsidize our prices with their lives.

The only person who can truly realize the outrageous injustice of having to sit by and watch a child slowly die of an easily preventable disease caused by malnutrition is the mother or father of that child. The only person who can truly realize the outrageousness of the injustice of having to sit and watch a person slowly die and suffer excruciating pain related to AIDS or TB is the person who knows and loves that person. While two thousand children die each week of diseases related to malnutrition, the twenty-five highest paid executives in the health care industry in the United States made a total of $201.1 million in annual compensation, not counting unexercised stock options, which were valued at $1.1 billion.[33] Isn't the system designed to include some and to leave many out? Don't the powerful take care of their children and turn their backs on the weak? Isn't there a relationship between billions of people without rights to basic health care and the tremendous wealth accumulated by health care executives and the drug companies?

Those of us with access to health care just cannot be expected to comprehend the brutality of a system that denies so many people access to health care. It is hard to imagine that approximately 1 billion people on earth have no access at all to modern health care. It is the powerful who decide who gets what, at what price, and who is left without health care. They decide who is left to suffer and die. This needless suffering and death is a type of violence. It is connected to the policies of the international financial institutions that result in cuts to health care for those dependent upon the resources of the ministries of health.

Lack of access to health care is not just a problem in the developing countries. In the United States over 45 million people are without health care insurance, and the number is growing. The United States is the only developed country in the world without universal health care. The powerful in Washington have not been able to agree on any method to provide health care to all. There is a link between political policy and poverty. Sick people who must spend more for medical bills may lose their homes and become homeless. Or they may suffer the illness and use the money to pay the rent or mortgage. Some families without health care go bankrupt because of medical bills.

Our political and economic structures could be organized to feed the hungry, to provide water for the thirsty, to care for the sick, and to educate all of the children. But the powerful, mostly men, have organized the current system. So most white people have food, water, access to health care, and education. But people of color and their children do not fare so well.

It is hard to accept the fact that so many precious people are without resources, especially health care, because of decisions made by the powerful. It is hard to accept that the powerful make calculated decisions which devastate the lives of so many people. It takes great courage to open one's heart and mind to the tremendous injustice and suffering in our world. However, unless we recognize the reality of suffering and injustice and the tremendous dichotomy between culture and gospel, there will be little incentive for hope, to respond and to love.

A poem written by Linda Panetta beautifully describes the precarious notion of the struggle of poor women and children throughout the world.

OUR MOTHER ... OUR SISTER

Can you imagine how far it had to travel ...
how long it's taken for that ray of sunlight to paint your
    face,
your sorrow, your love that way?

Gentle woman, beautiful child,
what pain you have felt ... the loneliness you've
    endured ...
the violence that you've known.
How you have grieved for the blood that has been shed,
for the innocence stolen away,
for the hopelessness that now consumes your soul.

Forgive me that I do not do more, do not know the best
    ways,
am not sensitive or humble enough.
Show me, teach me, be One with me
my beloved Mother, my Sister, my friend.

— "Mayan Blessing" and Poetry by Linda Panetta
www.soawne.org/OurMother.html

Chapter 10

Violence against Latino Workers in El Salvador and the United States

Much of the violence that faces workers in Central America today has roots in the tumultuous times of the 1960s and 1970s, when communism was seen by the United States as a global threat to democracy and freedom. Leftist or revolutionary movements, particularly that of Castro in Cuba, were seen as alarming signs that communism was actively encroaching on American territory. The CIA and lesser-known government agencies were actively involved in countering these movements in both South and Central America. They used many means, including arming and training paramilitaries, such as the Contras of Nicaragua. I now realize that in my efforts to establish credit unions in Venezuela and to investigate the conditions of workers in El Salvador, I too was unwittingly part of this process.

After graduating from college, I joined the Peace Corps and was assigned to Venezuela, where I helped labor unions form their own credit unions. When I arrived in Venezuela in 1964, a fellow Peace Corps volunteer and I were contacted by a representative of the United States Information Agency (USIA), who put us in touch with a group of workers from the Union of Telecommunication and Postal Workers who said they wanted to start a credit union. We assumed they were elected union representatives, but it turned out that they intended to use the credit union to gain control of the union itself. It never occurred to me that the USIA might be a front for the CIA. I was very surprised to learn much later that the CIA had actually had a hand in my Peace Corps work with credit unions.

That connection was made for me by a cousin who lived in Washington, DC, and whose husband worked at the White House. I was surprised, to say the least, to find out that I had been a tool of the CIA in helping it try to gain a foothold in the union closest to the communication system in Venezuela. Similar activities were taking place throughout Latin America.

In El Salvador in the early 1980s, for example, the great majority of unions were associated with leftist confederations of labor. The goal of the U.S. government (and the transnationals) was to create a new confederation of labor that would be aligned with U.S. interests. The goal was accomplished, but only after much struggle and a bloodbath of the former labor leaders. Then the new labor representatives, now favorable to U.S. interests, were brought to testify before the U.S. Congress to ask for military support to put down the revolution.

Eventually I learned how to pull back the layers of agencies to discover what lay at the core. An organization called the American Institute for Free Labor Development (AIFLD) was founded in the early 1960s by the U.S. government, the AFL-CIO, and U.S.-based multinationals that did business in Latin America. AIFLD was really a CIA-controlled labor center financed through the Agency for International Development. It was the force that created El Salvador's new labor confederation and that set a direction for what happened during the 1980s and the 1990s, and still happens even today. It is now known as the American Center for International Labor Solidarity.

In 1990 I served in El Salvador as an occupational safety and health consultant for the State Department's Agency for

International Development (AID) to evaluate a program related to the prevention of worker injury and disease. The program was designed to provide occupational safety and health consultation services to companies by having inspectors identify and recommend controls for workplace hazards. I was now far less innocent about the forces at play than I was as a Peace Corps volunteer.

The assumption underlining the AID-supported project was that labor, management, and government share the common goal of preventing worker injury, disease, and death. By having safety inspectors identify hazards and by recommending feasible controls, worker injury and death would be reduced. My evaluation first considered the design of the political, legal, and economic structures to see if they created incentives for industrialists to spend the money to control hazards. I interviewed more than a dozen owners of major corporations and the heads of manufacturing and employer associations and asked: What is the economic reason for a decision maker to spend money to control hazards? I found significant hazards in many of their workplaces, such as exposure to lead, asbestos, solvents, and other toxins likely to cause cancer, lung disease, lead poisoning, birth defects, central nervous system disorders, and so on. I found many machine hazards, as well as electrical and material handling hazards likely to result in amputation, paralysis, brain damage, or death. I asked: What economic incentive is there for you to spend the money to install ventilation systems, guard machines, and control other hazards when the controls have significant costs and sometimes slow down production? I never really expected a good answer because I knew that the political, economic, and legal structures were designed to create economic "disincentives" to control workplace hazards. The fact that the United States has political, economic, and legal structures that do indeed create incentives to control hazards is one

V. Gallagher

Unguarded chain and sprockets in a factory in Lima, Peru.

of the reasons the corporations have moved to Latin America and Asia.

In the United States, labor unions fought for the passage of workers' compensation laws and the Occupational Safety and Health Act (OSHA). When a worker is injured, he or she is entitled to receive compensation for medical expenses and lost wages. The employer must pay workers' compensation premiums for this injury. When the injury rate goes up, so does the premium. So it makes economic sense to control hazards to reduce workers' compensation premiums. Likewise, with the passage of the Occupational Safety and Health Act in 1970, employers could be fined if during unannounced inspections they were found to violate safety and health standards. The threat of fines created economic incentive for employers to control hazards. We also have common law whereby injured workers can sue a "third party" such as the manufacturer of an industrial machine or equipment that is unsafely designed or without adequate warning. In the construction industry, an injured worker may be able to sue the general contractor or a subcontractor for negligence that led to injury. These laws have created economic incentive to prevent worker injury. In El Salvador, and indeed all of Latin America, there is little incentive to control workplace hazards because the employer does not have to pay the full cost of the injury. Instead of workers' compensation in Latin America there is social security. Social security does pay for medical expenses and a percentage of the lost wages of the injured worker. But the problem is that the employer pays the social security administration a fixed premium dependent upon the number of workers on the payroll and not dependent on the costs of injuries of a particular employer. Social security does not provide economic incentives for the employer because no matter how many workers are injured or sickened, the social security premium is the same.

The Ministry of Labor in El Salvador performs safety inspections and theoretically has power to fine — but hardly ever does. When it does, the fines are very small. The politicians control the bureaucrats so the inspectors have no clout and pose no threat to employers. And there simply is no common law in Latin America that gives workers the right to sue.

When I asked some Latin American industrialists about economic incentives, I was curious to see what their answers would be. At first, some made very unconvincing arguments about how it is just good business. Some understood right away what I was getting at. None gave any good "economic" reason to control hazards. All eventually said something to the effect that it is ethical or moral to prevent worker injury and disease. But the fact is that with an abundant and docile labor force it is less expensive to simply replace injured workers than to spend the money to control the hazards.

Before leaving El Salvador, I had to give a briefing of my evaluation. I pointed out to the AID representatives that their project was essentially doomed to fail because of the "structural" impediments inherent in the system. At one point in my briefing I said, "Moral exhortations to the oligarchy have not been successful." I was told quickly and emphatically by the head of the group that I should "watch my language." I said: "Sir, I have watched my language. I had written that moral exhortations to the oligarchy have resulted in priests having their brains blown out, nuns being raped and killed, students disappearing, and labor reps being killed." I told him that I changed the report because I thought that some people might be offended. I did not get any more work from the State Department.

The differences in the political, economic, and legal structures in El Salvador compared with those of the United States explain in part why U.S.-based corporations have relocated to Latin America. But they do not explain why Latino workers in the United States often do not get the same legal protection that others receive.

Institutionalized Violence against Latino Workers in the United States

According to the National Day Labor Study published in January 2006, on any given day approximately 117,600 workers are either working for or are employed as day laborers in the construction industry as carpenters, roofers, painters, and drywall installers, in gardening and landscaping, as farm workers, cleaners, movers, in child care, in restaurants, and so on. Eighty percent of the day laborers are from Central America or Mexico. Nearly half of all day laborers had been completely denied payments in the two months prior to the survey. Similarly 48 percent were found to be underpaid; 28 percent were insulted or threatened by employers; 27 percent were abandoned at the work site by the employer; and 18 percent were subjected to direct violence by their employers.[1] All of that abuse occurred within the two months prior to the interview. While the day labor market is rife with employer abuse, none is more severe than being exposed to workplace hazards.

An Associated Press investigation found that hazards facing Mexican workers in the United States claim the life of a worker every day. They die cutting tobacco in North Carolina, cutting beef in Nebraska, cutting trees in Colorado, trimming grass in California, falling from roofs in New Jersey, being crushed in collapsing trenches, being crushed in machinery, and so on.[2] The Occupational Safety and Health Administration of the Department of Labor has found that 95 to 99 percent of the time, the death has resulted from noncompliance with an OSHA regulation that would have prevented the fatal injury.[3]

Deaths from Falls — Residential Construction

Because the residential construction industry has been booming, owners and investors have been making a substantial profit. However, many immigrant construction workers who are in great demand have not fared so well. In 2002, more Mexican workers died of fatal falls in the construction industry than from any other cause. Many others have suffered paraplegia, quadriplegia, brain damage, or death.

Since 1971, the Occupational Safety and Health Administration has been requiring residential builders to implement occupational safety and health programs to comply with safety standards related to fall protection. However, it takes time to work safely. Because time is money, frequently decisions are made by builders to save money, even at the risk of endangering workers' lives. It is very rare for an immigrant framer or roofer to have received the proper training related to fall protection, and it is rare that they use reliable fall protection while working at heights.

When a worker falls from a roof or through an unguarded stairway opening, the general subcontractor may be sued by the injured worker for not requiring the contractor to install fall protection. Workers in the United States are prohibited from suing their employers, except in very unusual circumstances. However, they can sue the general contractor if the general contractor's negligence led to the injury. In order to avoid the cost of a lawsuit the general contractor often requires the subcontractor to sign a contract with an "indemnification" or "save harmless" clause, which requires the subcontractor's insurance company to pay for the cost if injury occurs. The general contractor may require the subcontractor to purchase liability insurance. So the general contractor is protected from economic harm but permits the worker to be exposed to physical harm. This is simply another method of institutionalizing violence.

There is also a good chance that an injured immigrant worker will not receive medical care. The National Day Labor Study found that more than half (54 percent) of day laborers who had been injured on the job did not receive medical care for their injury. They found that only 6 percent of injured day laborers had medical expenses covered by their employer's workers' compensation. The employers simply deny coverage or threaten the worker with nonpayment of wages or other forms of retaliation should they attempt to file a workers' compensation claim.[4] It is easy for the general contractor or builder to get away with violating the law because there are so few OSHA inspectors. There are fewer than three thousand OSHA inspectors but some forty-nine thousand fish and game wardens in the United States. Even if OSHA investigates the fatal accident, the fine will likely be minimal. And the great majority of the time OSHA fails to fine the builder even though administrative procedures say it should. OSHA is also supposed to pursue willful violations of its standards that result in death, but it rarely does. OSHA, like all regulatory agencies, is affected by the "political wind."

Temporary Labor Agencies

Immigrant workers are often employed by temporary labor agencies. They are sent to work in a factory and paid minimum wage or just a bit more. The factory owner finds it is cheaper to use workers from the temporary agencies than to pay all of the federal, state, and workers' compensation costs normally associated with labor costs of workers on the payroll. When temporary workers get injured, they may be threatened by a representative of the temporary labor agency with being reported to immigration and being sent back to their country of origin if they file a workers' compensation claim or lawsuit. These workers are the most desperate and compliant of workers in the United States. They will rarely complain of being exposed to workplace hazards, although they are often exposed to risks of serious or catastrophic injury. Examples of recent injuries suffered by immigrant workers due to violations of OSHA standards include:

* An immigrant worker was shredded in an unguarded fan in a factory just outside of Philadelphia.

* A worker suffered hand amputation in a bakery in Camden, New Jersey.

* A worker suffered quadriplegia after being struck by a load that fell from a forklift in northern New Jersey.

◆ A worker fell from a roof and suffered brain damage in Camden County, New Jersey.[5]

Many workers, immigrant, minority, and others, are required to work while exposed to a variety of industrial toxins, fall hazards, machine hazards, electrical hazards, and so on. Industrial decision makers usually know of the dangers in their workplace but decide not to spend the money to control the hazard. When a worker suffers amputation, lung disease, cancer, a heart attack, or heat stroke, that is violence. It is institutionalized because the political, economic, and legal system is designed so that when the worker is catastrophically injured, sickened, or killed, the culprits very often do not have to pay the full cost of the injury, disease, or death. Instead of the system providing incentives for industrial decision makers to prevent immigrant worker injury, it provides "disincentives." For there to be incentive to prevent injury, the primary culprit, the builder, should be required to pay the full costs of injuries. As the system and contracts are designed, those costs are shifted to the workers, their families, and to the hospitals if treatment is given. The culprit gets a "free ride" on the backs of the workers, families, and hospitals. This is institutionalized violence.

The United States has a long history of taking advantage of immigrant labor. Our ancestors built the rails, the skyscrapers, and the dams, worked in slaughterhouses and factories. Children worked in the mines and the mills. But over the years through their unions, workers fought for the end of child labor, and for the enforcement of safety and health protection laws. Such laws are now in place and should provide justice to all workers, including the recently arrived.

Chapter 11

The Need for a Theology That Liberates

Theology can be practiced and lives can be lived without concern for issues of justice. A theology that considers suffering as a condition to be endured before going back to God in death will not question the causes of unjust suffering. A theology that concerns itself only with following the rules, family values, and personal spiritual growth may ignore issues of justice altogether. In the 1960s, theologians in Latin America began to question the injustice inherent in their political, legal, and economic systems. They began to question the way theology was thought of and practiced.

The theology of liberation began in the early 1960s in Latin America where there are many, many poor people, very few rich people, and not much of a middle class in most countries. Father Gustavo Gutiérrez in Peru and other Catholic and Protestant theologians throughout Latin America began seeing the inequities in Latin America in light of the gospel, which led to their formulation of a theology of liberation. They began to see the political, legal, and economic structures that dominate and oppress the poor for the benefit of the rich as *sinful structures.*

The notion of "institutionalized violence" was expressed in the Second Plenary Meeting of the Latin American Bishops' Conference held in Medellín, Colombia, in 1968. Latin American

Young girls in El Salvador.

bishops called for Christians to be involved in the transformation of society and to denounce "institutionalized violence" and structural injustice. Theologians began to see theology that focuses solely on religious dogma and abstract religious concepts as increasingly irrelevant to daily life. They began to question how to be Christian in a society that tolerates and even supports great inequity. They began to question the emphasis of traditional theology on charity, which actually supports the status quo, rather than on justice. Gustavo Gutiérrez defined theology as a "critical reflection on praxis [learning by reflection on experience] in the light of the word of God."[1] Liberation theology recognizes the need for liberation from oppressive structures, whether they be political, economic, social, sexual, or religious.

Liberation theology sees the role of the church as identifying with the dispossessed and the poor, witnessing their suffering, accompanying them in their struggle to confront their oppressors and gain liberation. It is also the role of the church to help the poor see and understand their oppression through the reading of scripture. The reign of God is not something that will come only after their lives end, but something that lies within all people. This is what Jesus taught about God's reign. It is at hand and it is manifest when we care for each other and lose ourselves in love.

Gutiérrez and other liberation theologians have examined the alleged "apolitical" attitude of Jesus presented by many traditional theologians, finding, to the contrary, that Jesus takes a stand. As a Jew, Jesus was aware of the Zealots, a Jewish nationalistic group that actively resisted the oppression of Rome. The Zealots eagerly awaited the reign of God because they believed it would end their subjugation. It is not surprising that the Zealots were attracted to Jesus. One of the disciples, Simon, was a Zealot. Jesus confronted the powerful Pharisees and Sadducees and the legalistic religious structures of the time by turning to the great prophets of Israel who taught that worship is authentic only when it is based on love rather than the law and on genuine commitment to others, especially the needy. It was this message of justice that was retrieved by the liberation theologians of Latin America.

Justice and the option for the poor was a major theme of the Latin American bishops' meeting in Medellín. The bishops called for Christians to be involved in the transformation of society and in denouncing "institutionalized violence" and structural injustice. This call reached ordinary people, including and especially the poor of Latin America, through the formation of base Christian communities (known also as small Christian communities). Led by trained lay persons, these communities were made up of small groups that met regularly to read the Bible and to interpret it in light of the struggles of their daily lives. The poor of

Latin America began to discover that the gospels are full of references of the great concern of God and Jesus for the poor and the oppressed.

Traditionally in Latin America most priests and church leaders preached resignation to God's will in a way that reinforced the notion that the way things are, including the distribution of wealth and power, comes from God. Suffering was simply a part of life, and believers would find their comfort in heaven. But liberation theologians called the clergy and the laity to give up relatively comfortable lives and go into the barrios and rural areas to live with the poor, to witness, to raise consciousness, to develop a sense of solidarity with the poor, and to consider the causes of poverty and social injustice. Voluntary poverty was seen as an act of love and solidarity with the poor and those who suffer from injustice.

Liberation theologians pointed out that a reading of scripture, and especially the gospels, from the point of view of the poor will likely mean something quite different from the interpretation of the wealthy and powerful. For example:

> Blessed are the poor in spirit, for theirs is the kingdom of heaven.
> Blessed are those who mourn, for they will be comforted.
> Blessed are the meek, for they will inherit the earth.
>
> — Matthew 5:3–5

A rich person may wonder, what is so blessed about being poor, meek, or mourning? A person who is poor may be better able to recognize Jesus' great compassion for people like them — without influence and suffering oppression. The poor understand the notion of the gospel's "preferential option of the poor" as they see their circumstances and struggles represented so often in the gospels.

Another reading from scripture often cited by liberation
theologians is from Isaiah:

> The spirit of the Lord God is upon me,
> because the Lord has anointed me;
> he has sent me to bring good news to the oppressed,
> to bind up the brokenhearted,
> to proclaim liberty to the captives,
> and release to the prisoners; to proclaim the year of
> the Lord's favor,
> and the day of vengeance of our God;
> to comfort all who mourn.   —Isaiah 61:1–2

For people living on less than two dollars a day this is good news.

The traditional prosperous church has focused on individual
and family faith with little emphasis on the biblical notion that
salvation involves liberation from oppressive economic and political structures as well. Bishop Dom Helder Camara of Brazil
is a good example of a bishop who embraced the theology of
liberation. He has said:

> Whoever is suffering, whether in body or soul; whoever is
> in despair, be he rich or poor, will have a special place in
> the heart of the bishop. But I have not come here to help
> anyone to delude himself into thinking that a little char-
> ity and social work will suffice. There is no doubt about
> it; there is a crying misery to which we have no right to
> remain indifferent. Very often, we have no choice but to
> take immediate action, however inadequate. But let us not
> deceive ourselves into thinking that the problem is limited
> to a few gestures of reform; let us not confuse the beauti-
> ful and indispensable idea of order, the end of all human
> progress, with the mockery of order which is responsible

for preserving structures we all know should not and cannot be preserved.... We bishops of the Northeast found we had no choice but to encourage the farm workers to organize into unions as the only practical way to enable them to discuss their rights with landowners.... We feel obliged to help rather than simply leave to laymen the work which would normally be a sign of Christian presence in the temporal world.... We feel the necessity to lend our moral support to the fundamental task of defending human rights. We must not commit a sin of omission. We cannot remain outside the struggle.[2]

At the time when liberation theology was emerging, others in Latin America were attempting to change the structures of oppression through violent means. In Cuba in the late 1950s, through bloody revolution, Castro established a communist state aligned with the Soviet Union. In the late 1970s in Nicaragua, the Sandinistas led a bloody revolution to overthrow Somoza, a ruthless dictator. The Sandinistas reportedly received support for their army from Cuba and the Soviet Union. Also in the 1970s, civil wars or revolutions were beginning in El Salvador and Guatemala.

A Time of Unrest in Latin America

In the 1970s and 1980s, there was great fear of revolution among the rich and powerful in Central America as well as in the United States, which had many corporations invested heavily in Latin America. In the late 1970s, leftists in El Salvador began to organize. Some students, workers, labor leaders, and others took up arms and began attacking government troops. They had hoped to attract others and to eventually overthrow the government. To prevent a revolution, the U.S. government began to give millions of dollars in aid to the El Salvadoran military. A great repression began.

The repression included the slaughter of peasants, workers, students, lawyers, doctors, teachers, intellectuals, journalists, human rights advocates, catechists, priests, religious sisters, and bishops. There were massacres of totally defenseless peasants. The total killed in El Salvador is estimated at seventy thousand.[3] In Guatemala, it is estimated at eighty thousand.[4]

In El Salvador, the repression began most notably with the murder of Jesuit Rutilio Grande and his two companions, a boy and an old man, on March 12, 1977. Father Grande's death had a great impact on Archbishop Oscar Romero. Romero had been a very conservative auxiliary bishop who had previously regarded some Jesuits as Marxists. However, with the death of Father Grande, his eyes and heart were opened to the injustice and suffering of the poor in El Salvador. He became more outspoken, and because of it, he received death threats. He knew his life was at risk. Just one month before he was killed, he declared: "If they kill me, I shall rise again in the Salvadoran people." In his last homily broadcast throughout El Salvador, he said: "In the name of God, then, and in the name of the suffering people, whose screams and cries mount to heaven, and daily grow louder, I beg you, I entreat you, I order you in the name of God — stop the repression!"[5] The next day, he was shot through the heart while celebrating Mass.

An endless procession of people suffered martyrdom. On December 2, 1980, Maura Clark, Ita Ford, Dorothy Kazel, and Jean Donovan, Catholic missionaries serving the poor in El Salvador, were raped and murdered. They had received death threats but could not be scared off.

One day students at the University of Central America (UCA) arrived to find fourteen left arms strewn across the street at the gate of the university. It was a message to the leftists. Rightists are the rich, industrialists, military, and government officials who support the status quo. Leftists are those who are active in caring for and supporting the poor, that is, human rights workers, labor representatives, students, environmentalists, community organizers, and others who accompany the poor.

In El Salvador, and indeed in many countries of the world, many students are leftists. Because of their idealism, they want to change society. In Latin America, students sometimes become politically active and form alliances with workers, human rights organizations, religious organizations, and political organizations that serve workers, women, children, and the poor. Some students from UCA were joining with rebels and taking up arms against the government. Thus the grim warning to the students.

On November 16, 1990, approximately thirty uniformed, armed men entered the home of the Jesuits on the campus of the University of Central America. They murdered Segundo Montes, Ignacio Martín-Boró, Amando López, Juan Ramón Moreno, Joaquín López y López, Julia Elba, their cook, and her fifteen-year-old daughter, Celina. They blew out the brains of the priests and laid them alongside their head, as a sign to other intellectuals. Father Jon Sobrino would have been killed with them, but he was teaching in Thailand.

In his book *Witnesses to the Kingdom,* Sobrino points out that poverty is increasing in Latin America, and the need for liberation theology is more urgent than ever. Liberation is needed from the death and torture produced by the military powers and the death squads; from the hunger produced by economic powers and the oligarchies; from the submissiveness and indignity produced by the political powers and rulers; from the lies produced by the powers of the communication media; from the evasions and justifications produced by the religious powers; from the infantilization produced by the powers of entertainment, and so on. Sobrino points out that the church has stopped speaking of transforming structures, of saving people, and of bringing in the kingdom of God. Instead it focuses on individual and family salvation rather than salvation of a people and historical salvation. Its activity is more charitable than liberating. It supports the weak but fails to confront the oppressor. He pleads with us to bring the Crucified Christ down from the cross; for this, Sobrino tells us, is the marrow of liberation theology.

Guatemala

During the 1970s in Guatemala, the Maryknoll sisters and priests trained over 350 catechists to form base communities in which the members read and considered the gospel in light of their daily struggles. Poor people in Guatemala could easily relate to the kingdom that Jesus spoke of so often. People throughout Latin America were beginning to see the injustice inherent in the political and economic structures that dominated their lives. They began to see the system as sinful. They saw the rich and the military who protected the rich as beneficiaries of a sinful society and themselves as the abused poor whom Jesus seemed to favor. They began to hunger for justice and sometimes demand their rights. Some took up arms to fight government troops. The powerful responded with repression. It began in earnest after President Ronald Reagan was elected in 1980. About five thousand Guatemalans had taken up arms to overthrow the government. Government troops responded by entering the villages to intimidate people to prevent an uprising. The first person killed was the catechist. All of the catechists trained by the Maryknollers and thousands of other Guatemalans were killed.[6]

The president of Guatemala at this time was Efraín Ríos Montt, a CIA-backed, U.S.-trained dictator. He was also an evangelical who espoused a fundamentalist theology that fo-cused on salvation after death rather than efforts to bring about justice by changing structures. When troops entered a village, the evangelicals were much less likely to be abused or killed than those who practiced a theology of liberation. People were rewarded for not getting involved in fighting for justice and ef-forts to change structures and for participating in a "pie in the sky when you die" theology.

Oppressive structures in poor countries lead to material poverty. The beneficiaries of the unjust structures sometimes un-knowingly suffer a spiritual poverty. They are sometimes blind to the tremendous injustice before them, and are attracted to a safe theology that does not disturb. They are likely to become more and more patriotic, concerned with family values and personal spiritual growth disconnected from true gospel values. Because of their blindness they can see the sins of others more clearly than their own. They do not recognize the "logs" in their eyes.

Chapter 12

Awakening to the Reality of Suffering

Never forget, my children, that the poor are our masters. That is why we should love them and serve them, with utter respect, and do what they bid us. — St. Vincent de Paul

Awakening is essential for spiritual growth. The Buddha taught that the first noble truth is to awaken to the reality of suffering in our midst. Jesus taught us to embrace the sick, the oppressed, the outcast, and those abandoned, that is, those who suffer the most. He showed us the way. He challenged those who held power over an oppressed people. He became the Way. He taught us that the way to the kingdom is through the cross — giving up your life for those you love.

An important step is to acknowledge the truth of the existence of suffering in our world and in ourselves. Without the recognition and acceptance of the reality of suffering, there is little hope. Paradoxically, once we accept the existence of suffering rather than denying its existence or numbing ourselves of its sting, hope then becomes possible. Awakening to the reality of suffering breaks our heart open. Then love is possible. When we love, we will naturally want to relieve suffering. Our efforts to relieve suffering will result in our own spiritual hunger being fed. As we gradually awaken, we realize our own spiritual hunger results from having too much while knowing of the tremendous material needs of others.

Through grace, prayer, and becoming deeply involved in the struggles of others and our own spiritual struggle, we gradually love more and awaken to this kingdom that is "at hand" and within us all. That message will not appear on TV or in the newspapers.

What will appear in the media are the values of competition, materialism, and consumerism. They have been ingrained into our psyches. Our minds have been colonized. We are inundated with TV commercials, sitcoms, talk shows, news reports, and commentaries that communicate to our children and all of us the predominant values of our media. Essentially, the media values sex, violence, money, thin bodies, wine and beer, athletes, rock stars, rappers, and the beautiful rich and famous people. We live in a consumer society where it seems most people really worship at our malls and sports stadiums. It is difficult, if not impossible, to shelter our children and ourselves from these values, which are diametrically opposed to spiritual values. They are truly seductive.

It is scandalous that our children are bombarded by these false values. Americans are on the top of the heap of wealth in the world. Most will never worry about having enough food, clothing, or shelter. Most have more economic security than 99 percent of the people who have ever inhabited the planet. Yet the media gets us focusing on what we do not have. The children don't stand a chance when the adults in their lives have been seduced by the predominant cultural values. We have to wake each other up. Our children know where Disney World is, but they don't know where Haiti is. Ask any class of fifth grade children, working class or middle class, how many have been to Disney World. You will find that almost all have. Many have been there two or three times. It is not that Disney World is bad; nor are music and musicians, wine and beer, cruises to Alaska, vacations to Cancun, gourmet restaurants, thin bodies, fashionable hair colors, clothes, investments for retirement, reliable cars, and so on. But can we overdo it? We now have health insurance for our pets, dog food designed for fresh breath and low fat, and hotels for dogs costing $80 to $125 per day. We have Hummers and cars with computers connected to satellites to give us directions to the nearest Thai restaurant no matter where we are. We have golf carts with computers that tell us exactly how many feet we are from the green at all times. I read of a man who paid $18,000 for his twelve-year-old Labrador retriever to receive an operation for cancer.

One time I was working in Las Vegas. When a worker was run over by a forklift, I had to testify in court. I was put up in the Flamingo Hotel. I had to meet with the lawyer at the Mirage Hotel the night before the trial to prepare. They actually have a rain forest in the lobby of the hotel. Outside the hotel there is an artificial waterfall that every hour becomes a "volcano" — spewing flames high in the air and making noises like an erupting volcano. People thought it was spectacular. People carried drinks and had containers of silver dollars strapped on their belts. Some men were handing out cards with pictures of women with telephone numbers and places to go to purchase sexual favors. There was a man with a big sign with Bible quotes on it, walking up and down, saying out loud, "Repent!" He was apparently mentally ill. But I wondered, Was he sicker than most? Like him, I was tempted to tap the people on their shoulders and say, "We've gone too far. No one knows it. Please tell the others. We've gone too far." The worst part about Las Vegas now is that the target population is families. The kids don't stand a chance.

Most of us have way too much, yet feel insecure and deprived. "They" have got us where they want us — afraid and wanting. As they say, you can't be too thin or have too much money.

Anorexia is a serious problem. A bigger problem is that most of us have too much to eat. Sixty percent of the people in Haiti are malnourished, yet we spend billions helping people not to eat too much. The arteries to our hearts are blocked by our overindulgence. Our hearts are being attacked. We don't love the oppressed because we don't know the oppressed, because most of us have bought the American dream hook, line, and sinker.

Nevertheless, some of us are awakening. One example is the work done by Jubilee 2000, an international church-based movement calling for cancellation of debt. In Birmingham, England, in 1998, seventy thousand people, many middle-aged churchgoers on their first demonstration, formed a human chain around the G7 Summit. The G7 (predecessor of G8) consisted of representatives of the most powerful countries in the world. Jubilee 2000 succeeded in forcing debt onto the agenda and won significant concessions at the G7 Summit in Cologne the following year.[1]

In July 2005, young people throughout the world were awakened by Live 8 concerts, which brought attention to the debt burden of the poorest African nations. In September of 2005 the G8 nations agreed to pay $42.5 billion of debt relief to the IMF/WB for eighteen of the poorest countries in Africa. Another example is the demonstrations at the School of Americas every year in November, where thousands of ordinary people come from all around the country to advocate and pray for justice. Likewise, there are massive demonstrations at the annual meetings of the international financial institutions such as those that have taken place in Seattle, Miami, Washington, Canada, Mexico, Brazil, Argentina, Venezuela, France, Germany, Italy, England, India, the Philippines, New Zealand, Australia, Kenya, South Africa, Thailand, Malaysia, and Indonesia.

Many regional and international solidarity groups have also been formed. The largest is the World Social Forum. It first met in 2001 in Porto Alegre, Brazil. It also met in January of 2004 in Mumbai, India. More than a hundred thousand people attended. Those in attendance were environmentalists, women's groups, movements to cancel debt, and movements opposed to free trade, militarization, sweatshops, and labor repression. It was attended by many indigenous people, including landless peasants and workers.

Marie Dennis of Maryknoll's Office of Global Concern has said: "People are doing the homework that helps them dig deeper and get closer to root causes. Congregations, parishes, students, and people across the United States made the most amazing effort to understand what the debt debate was all about — and they got it. Very subtle issues became comfortable language for parish groups that had no expertise and really weren't all that interested a few years ago."[2]

What Keeps Us Stuck?

The American Dream

All cultures have their myths and stories. In America, we have the Horatio Alger myth, the frontier, pioneer, cowboy myths, and most of all the American dream. We all have our own story to live, our own history to create. Some live the story dreamed up for them by others. In America, success is primarily measured in dollars. Most of us have some expectation of the type of car we would like to drive, the neighborhood where we would like to live, the type of spouse we would like to marry, the number of children we would like to have, the type of job we would like to have, the amount of money we would like to earn, and so on. In our materialistic, consumer society, we have been programmed since birth in many subtle and not so subtle ways to want the American dream. We cannot help but have these expectations.

Some figure that after they fulfill the American dream and have all they need, they will then have the time, energy, and perhaps money to devote to service in the world beyond their immediate families. So they put off the call to live the authentic life of the hero. Their story is lived out in their own little world. They seek secure, well-paying jobs and live in gated communities rather than venturing into the wild to slay dragons. They dare not journey to the Land of Oz. They dream safe, small dreams.

It takes tremendous courage to live authentically and to try to hear that call from your heart to live and love deeply in your own special way. It takes tremendous courage not to follow the crowd and to turn your back on the American dream.

Fear of Pain

We all tend to seek pleasure and avoid pain, to seek safety and avoid risk and danger. Yet eventually we all get hurt. All of our hearts get broken and shattered in different ways. The pain can be tremendous. Children can be very cruel to each other. We all have been ridiculed, rejected, and betrayed. Many have been abused, battered, or raped. Many of us have been shamed and have done shameful things. We have all hurt others and been hurt by others. To avoid pain, we close our hearts and reinforce ourselves with distractions, pleasures, addictions, and destructive behaviors of all kinds. Our wounds cause us to disconnect. They awaken feelings of helplessness and powerlessness. They cause us to drop illusions about life and who we think we are.

It takes tremendous courage to face the pain, shame, and mistakes we have made in our lives. If we deny them or push them under, they will eventually fester and resurface. They may cause us to hurt others by our projections of what is denied.

"Hurt" people hurt people

Until all of the hurt in us is met in the light of acceptance, understanding, love, compassion, and forgiveness, we will remain disconnected. Until we have attained some understanding and acceptance of our own helplessness and powerlessness, we will never be able to understand or feel the pain of others. We will not want to be with others in a way that involves entering their pain and powerlessness.

Righteousness and Charitable Activities

Some get stuck because of their righteousness. Deep down, they feel they are really good people. Blessed with loving parents, they are intelligent and are aware more than most of the injustice in the world. Perhaps they pray for the poor, give generously to the church, worship often, perform meaningful work, and serve a day or two a month at a soup kitchen or nursing home. And they have no realization whatsoever of their own poverty.

Some righteous people think of the poor as the uneducated, unsophisticated, oppressed, and disenfranchised minority. So they give money, food, and clothing out of pity and without humility. They see no connection between themselves and those oppressed. They have no relationship with those whom they serve. They end up with heavy "golden chains" around their necks and never really learn to love.

Fear, Comfort, and Laziness

Some are stuck because they are lazy and too comfortable. Some are afraid to take chances. It takes courage to enter the camp of the "other" where you are a stranger. You may ask: Why would I do such a thing? What will I say? What will I do? What will people think of me? Why am I really thinking of doing this? Some feel it is just too dangerous to go into that kind of neighborhood.

Besides, there are parties to go to, ball games to watch, and plenty of other things to do with your spare time.

It takes courage to do things that your friends don't do, to be a stranger, to enter a new culture, to be unsure of what you will say and of what you will do. Some just want to play it safe and not face those kinds of risks. They want what is familiar and secure. Taking comfort in safety is the best they will do. The desire for comfort and economic security are perhaps the greatest impediments to spiritual growth in America.

Guilt

Some get stuck in guilt and prefer it rather than entering into the pain of others where they may be forced to examine their own pain or perhaps their own role in the structures that benefit them and oppress others. Some may take solace in confession and the announcement of forgiveness delivered each Sunday and so avoid entering the agony of the pain in the broken parts of others and themselves. It is far easier to pray for forgiveness, to pray for the poor, to give money, or to write letters to politicians on behalf of the poor rather than getting in touch with broken people and broken parts of yourself.

Lack of Imagination

Some just can't imagine living a life greater than the American dream. They can't imagine themselves living the life of a hero, warrior, adventurer, prophet, or saint. They can't imagine themselves protecting the weak, rescuing the endangered, defending the rights of the oppressed, or speaking truth to power. They see themselves as little people, cogs in the wheel, without power, without voice, and without great compassion, love, and integrity. They are safe without dreams. When the opportunity to respond, to speak out, to act with great courage and integrity presents itself, they let the moment pass because they just never expected, hoped, or dreamed that they could do such a thing. I remember a line from "Happy Talk" in *South Pacific*. "If you don't have a dream, how you gonna have a dream come true?" We become the person whom we expect to become. When we imagine and believe, we set in motion something mysterious within and outside of ourselves. It is linked to the mystery of faith. As Goethe puts it, "There is one elemental truth, the ignorance of which kills countless ideas and splendid plans: the moment one definitely commits oneself then Providence moves, too. All sorts of things occur to help one that never otherwise would have occurred.... Whatever you can do or dream you can do, begin it. Boldness has genius, power, and magic in it. Begin it now."

Awakening Consciousness

In the 1960s in the United States, women began awakening to the various ways that they were treated unjustly by men and the organizations men created. They began to raise their consciousness about oppression and abuse in many ways. Women got together and evaluated the ways that men and the structures of power exercised control over their lives. They began to organize and confront the people, organizations, and laws that did not treat them fairly. A new, more energized women's movement began and is still at work today.

Some men in America are just awakening to how the system oppresses them and to the "bill of goods" sold to them by the powerful. Some honor the corporation more than their family by working long hours to compete and "be successful." Some will not question the government's policy on war because they have been taught that "a man's got to do what a man's got to do." Some close their hearts because they learned long ago that "big boys don't cry." When I ask teenage boys how they feel about a certain injustice, they almost invariably begin to answer by saying "I think ... " They do not understand the question. Neither do many of their fathers. The boys become like their dads. Ask eighth grade boys what they want to do when they grow up and most will answer, "I want to make a lot of money." They got the message. Men have much to learn from the women.

In developed countries, people are awakening and small groups are forming to examine issues of spirituality and justice. Any honest reading of the Bible and discussion of spiritual growth will result in questions of how to respond to unjust suffering in our midst. Some groups are content with examining questions of personal morality, family values, and traditional religious practice, but they will not examine the dichotomy of relatively rich Christians living in a world of great hunger. They will not consider questions of how they use their money and will have difficulty in understanding gospel themes that are quite apparent to people who are poor, for example, what Jesus meant by:

+ Don't store up riches here on earth.

+ Blessed are the meek, the poor, and those who mourn.

+ Those rejected are the cornerstone.

+ The last will be first and the first will be last.

+ Whoever wants to be first must be a servant of all.

+ How difficult it is for the rich to get into heaven.

However, there are faith groups that are courageously examining their lifestyles and the structural injustice that supports them. They are coming together and forming alliances with people in poor communities. Many parishes have formed sister-parish relationships with communities in Mexico and Central America. The Twinning Parish Program in Haiti has linked more than four hundred parishes in the United States with more than four hundred parishes in Haiti. Church- and faith-based organizations have been taking small groups in the United States to visit, serve, and learn from communities in Latin America. After visiting communities in poor countries, people in the United States and Europe have organized development projects involving water delivery, clinics, agricultural projects, education, and so on. They have also organized projects to sell handcrafts made by Third World people at fair prices. The concept of "fair trade" is beginning to take root and now includes coffee and is expanding to chocolate, fruit, and other products. Principles of fair trade include the following:

- Producers are paid a fair price and workers a fair wage. For crops like coffee, tea, and bananas, farmers are paid a stable minimum price.

- The links between buyers and sellers are shortened, doing away with the "middlemen."

- Buyers and producers develop long-term relationships of mutual support and benefit.

- All aspects of trade relationships are open to public accountability.

- Exploitive child labor and forced labor are prohibited.

- Working conditions are healthy and safe.

- Goods are produced and crops grown in an environmentally sustainable way.

"Millions and millions of Americans are now learning about fair trade through their places of worship. I don't think the value of that can be overestimated," said Rodney North of Equal Exchange, a for-profit cooperative in Massachusetts that has marketed fair trade products since 1986.[3] The Evangelical Lutheran Church of America has set a goal of purchasing 90 tons of fair trade coffee this year. Over the last five years, Transfair USA, a fair trade certifying organization in California, has provided small coffee producers with $34 million more than they would have earned by selling their crops through conventional channels.

Examples of organizations facilitating fair trade include:

+ Equal Exchange, a worker-owned co-op: *www.equalexchange.com*

+ Cooperative Trading, a not-for-profit membership organization: *www.friendsofthethirdworld.org*

+ Global Exchange, a human rights organization with campaigns around fair trade coffee: *www.globalexchange.org/coffee*

+ The Catholic Relief Services Coffee Project: *www.crsfairtrade.org*

+ Ten Thousand Villages, a nonprofit program of the Mennonite and Brethren in Christ Churches of America, with retail outlets in thirty-four states: *www.tenthousandvillages.org*

+ Wild Oats Markets, Inc.: *www.wildoats.com*

+ Interfaith Coffee Program: *www.equalexchange.com/interfaith*

+ No Sweat Apparel — Sale of union-made and sweatshop-free casual clothing: *www.nosweatapparel.com*

+ Catholic Relief Services Free-Trade Chocolate Project: *www.crsfairtrade.org*

Joining Hands Against Hunger is a church-based network that has brought together people from La Oroya, Peru, with people from Herculaneum, Missouri. A U.S.-based company, Doe Run, has smelters in each city. The smelting process results in emissions of sulfur dioxide and lead. In Herculaneum, contamination is captured by emission control technology — but not in La Oroya. People from Herculaneum became active in pressuring both in the United States and in Peru for equal protection from health hazards for people in La Oroya. They testified before the Peruvian Congress, urging passage of legislation that would require the same protection that people in the United States have.

The Spirit of Christ Catholic Church in a suburb of Denver makes connections with the poor in other countries in several ways. Fourteen percent of Sunday collection goes to the poor. In this upper-class parish, this amounts to $300,000 per year. Recipients of their aid include groups digging wells in Nicaragua, those providing care for AIDS orphans in Africa, and those serving the homeless. In their "southern exposure" program, forty groups of parishioners have constructed 150 homes in poverty-stricken areas of Mexico. Eight hundred parishioners participate in eighty small faith groups that discuss how the Sunday lectionary reading relates to their life in the world. There are four hundred people involved in liturgical and other ministries. The parish's adult education forum brings in high caliber guest speakers like Sister Helen Prejean and Bishop Thomas Gumbleton.[4]

Religious communities sometimes purchase small amounts of stock in target corporations and advocate for specific measures of justice. The Interfaith Center on Corporate Responsibility has 275 faith-based institutional members, who have filed 185 socially motivated shareholder resolutions with 130 U.S. and Canadian companies. Investors include national denominations, religious communities, pension funds, endowments, hospital corporations, economic development funds, and publishing companies. The combined portfolio value of the center's membership organizations is estimated to be $110 billion (*www.iccr.org*).

Some Catholic schools purchase skirts and blouses from a women's cooperative in Thailand where there is little women's work available and the sex trade flourishes.[5]

In the United States, as in Latin America, there are many small groups forming to discuss their spiritual lives. There is greater hope when two or more gather. Perhaps more prophets will be born in the discussions of people yearning for spiritual liberation who honestly and courageously examine their own spiritual poverty. Perhaps we will begin to see the spiritual oppression inherent in our society that favors money, sex, and power over poverty, chastity, and obedience.

Mother Teresa attended a fund-raiser in a Beverly Hills hotel organized to support her work. A woman asked her what she thought of the beautiful display in the hall and the wonderful food prepared for the guests. She answered that America is the poorest country in the world.

It is really hard for us to imagine the kingdom of God because the kingdom of Caesar has been drummed into our psyches. Certainly we know that the coming of God's reign on earth must be more than abundant material wealth and indulgence in the pleasures of life. There is nothing wrong with money or any of the pleasures, in moderation at the right time and place. All of the pleasures are meant to help us live, love, and enjoy the precious life given to us. The coming of the reign of God involves awakening to this kingdom that is before us and within us, all of us. We have to wake each other up.

Chapter 13

How We Can Respond

We are all *really* God's children. We have been dreamt by God to spend time here on earth, to awaken to the kingdom that is before us and within us, and to love. Earth is truly "crammed with heaven," as Emily Dickinson said. We are all here to love, to care for, to feed, to teach, and to protect each other.

No People More Precious Than Others

Dorothy Day, founder of the Catholic Worker, has said that all of our work is a "work of mercy." That is, mother, father, bus driver, mechanic, secretary, teacher, sister, priest, nurse, doctor, gardener: by the grace of God, we care for each other and hold each other together in many ways. We are called to give of the gifts we have been given. The only thing we take with us from this life is what we have given away.

Joseph Campbell has told thousands of college students to "follow their bliss," to live their dreams — not the roles prescribed by family or society. Too many, Campbell tells us, have spent their lives climbing to the top of their ladder only to find they placed it against the wrong wall. When they realize it, it is too late: they have a mortgage to pay and children in college. They spent their lives living their father's or their mother's dream or chasing the American dream and forgot how their heart ached as a young woman or young man. It takes courage to follow your

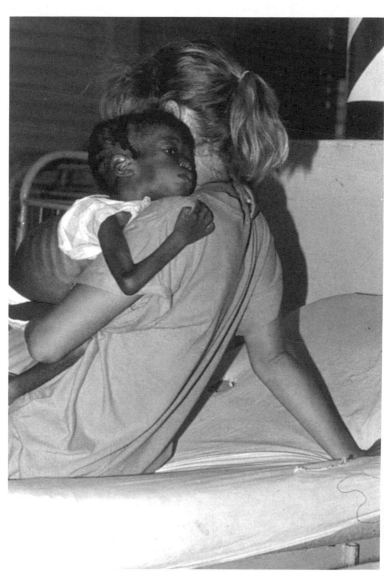

Loving a child in Haiti.

Mev Puleo

heart, to take your own counsel, to listen to your unique story, to live your life authentically.

Many Americans just do not know how much power they have to respond to the tremendous needs of so many people who suffer so much in so many ways. The problem is that many don't even know the name of anyone who is desperately poor. They don't know the name of anyone dying of starvation, working at the garbage dump, or in need of medical care so their child will not die. They have never talked with the lonely in a nursing home or prison. They don't know the name of a bright child with no access to education. And so they do not have the will or the know-how to connect. Americans do respond generously when they know who suffers and how they suffer. The problem is we do not know.

As I was preparing to do research on organizations that readers might consider when searching for ways to get involved in serving people suffering injustice and oppression, I did a search on the Internet for globalization/justice. There were literally millions of sites. People are already organized and doing things of value. Finding organizations doing good work is easy. Finding the best way to be involved will probably come from experience. A good first step is to look for opportunities to meet people who suffer injustice. If we stay in our small communities and never get to meet the oppressed person, we will probably never awaken to the tremendous injustices around us. However, if we have the courage to reach out to the oppressed, we will find that there is tremendous power in the encounter. It can cause a transformation within, leading to compassionate action. It can change the face of the earth.

It is very natural that one would not want to go into a very poor neighborhood in the United States or in a poor country. First there is the fear of violence. We think we will be a target and may be robbed. We are not used to being the stranger, and we do not understand the culture or the language. We feel uncomfortable on someone else's turf. It is scary. We wonder what we will say, what we will do, how we will be received, what they will think. Why am I really doing this and what will my friends think?

Most who have journeyed into poor communities are wonderfully surprised to find that they are almost always welcomed with open arms. Missionaries invariably relate that they were not only welcomed with great hospitality, but found that they had much to learn from the people they went to serve. They often say they found great faith, hope, generosity, and humility among the poor. There is a wonderful, powerful conversion and transformation that frequently takes place in the encounter.

Romero Center, Camden, New Jersey

The Romero Center, located in Camden, New Jersey, is one of many organizations that facilitate encounters of high school and college students and other groups with oppressed people (*www.romero-center.org*). Students visit with, listen to, and serve alongside residents in Camden, one of the poorest cities in the United States. They visit with people living with AIDS and teach children in preschool programs. They serve in soup kitchens, eat meals with Hispanic or African American families. They get in touch with people who have never had the opportunities that they have had. They also learn of the structural injustice that leads to poverty. The encounter often results in a powerful transformation. There are many organizations that facilitate encounters of middle-class people with people struggling for justice in developing countries. These encounters can be life-changing experiences.

The most powerful encounters that I have experienced have been in Haiti. Every year I visit Haiti to serve at the Home for

Malnourished Children or the House of the Destitute and Dying of the Missionaries of Charity, Mother Teresa's sisters. The experiences are powerful. It is truly a loving encounter. At the Home for Malnourished Children, I simply hold, feed, caress, and give massages to desperately sick children, many dying of AIDS. The experience is truly heartbreaking. It breaks your heart open and makes you love like you never knew you could.

On one visit, I met Milliata, a little girl who appeared to be six or seven years old but was actually twelve. She was dying of AIDS. She was close to the end when I saw her on the day I first arrived. I was able to give her massages as she lay in the crib. She was too weak to walk. She was skin and bones. All week long, I paid special attention to her. On Friday when I came back from lunch, I saw that her intravenous tube had been taken out. Milliata was put in a crib in a utility room to die. The sisters and the women who work at the center do not have time to sit for hours or days with a dying child. There are too many other children to care for. There was a bowl of blood under her crib. She must have recently vomited, for she had blood in her nostrils and around her mouth. She wanted to be taken out of the crib and held her arms up to me. I asked one of the women if it would be okay if I took her for a walk. She said it was okay. I sat with her in a rocking chair and tried to give her a massage. But after a short while, she didn't want the massage. I walked out back where it was a little cooler. She did not want to be outside, and she didn't want to be with me or anyone. She was angry, and she knew that she was dying. Most children do not realize that they are dying, but the older ones sometimes do. It was about time for me to leave so I put Milliata back in her crib. She didn't want to go back. She knew she would never get out. She had her arms raised to me and was crying. I did not realize she was so close to the end. If I had, I would have stayed with her. As I walked home that day, I never felt more sorrowful in my life.

When I arrived the next morning, I learned that Milliata had died. There was a short prayer service for her. Shortly thereafter, six desperately ill, tiny children were admitted. They weighed about ten pounds each. At the end of that day, I was the only volunteer left in the room with the six children. Three of them needed to be fed. The women in charge gave me three bowls. I knelt alongside the crib of the first child and fed him. The children were really hungry and they ate quickly. The little ones never took their big eyes off me while I fed them. As I fed each child, I heard the words of Jesus when he asked Peter: "Peter, do you love me?" Peter answered: "You know I love you, Lord." Jesus asked him again and again and he replied that he loved him, again and again. And each time he told Peter to feed his sheep.

The words of scripture were being prayed in me as I fed each child. Tears rolled down my face. With each spoon, I said, "I love you." The word became flesh there right before me. I was never the same.

One evening at the Romero Center while I was showing slides, I showed an image of a lady in Guatemala who suffered from arthritis and was not able to walk. She lived in a one-room shack with her two little daughters and her son. She was confined to her bed. I explained that she and literally a billion people like her simply have no access to medical care and try to survive on less than one dollar a day. I told them that I have some arthritis but simply take some Aleve when it gets bad. A young man spoke out and said simply and sincerely that he would like to visit her and bring her some Aleve. I told him that impulses like that, acted upon, can change the world. When we see some simple thing that we can do, we should just do it. Simple acts of kindness are tremendously powerful. Mother Teresa saw a dying person on the streets of Calcutta and had to do something. She knew she could do something to ease his death. And indeed she did. She then went on to help others rescue tens of thousands throughout the world and became a saint in the process. Through grace, as we grow in awareness and love, we will "see" the suffering souls and find unlimited ways to rescue them. Perhaps through grace we will come to see Jesus in his most distressing disguises, as Mother Teresa was able to see.

Because so many precious people suffer so much in so many ways, it is easy for us to do great good for many people. We have tremendous power because of our blessings of good health, education, money, and the ability to serve through our talents. We do not have to be physicians or missionaries, nor do we need to go to Haiti. Throughout the United States, there are precious lonely souls in nursing homes, living on the streets and in prisons. There are abused women and children in shelters, people with little food, elderly with houses falling apart, poor mothers in desperate need of baby sitters, people living and dying with AIDS. When Mother Teresa was asked what we in the developed countries should do, she always responded that we should begin in our own home. There probably is someone in your family who needs to be listened to and understood. God knows we all have our crosses.

Deep love has been planted at our center from birth. It is like a treasure in a field. It is like the yeast that causes the bread to rise. It is like the tiniest of seeds that grows and grows. We have all been called, chosen, and sent to love in our own special way. So gradually through the grace of God, prayer, and our growing desire to love, we will find unlimited ways to spend ourselves for each other.

The fire of the Holy Spirit is ignited when, through our contact with people in great need, the spiritual hunger within us is fed. A spiritual poverty grows in us when we close ourselves up, isolate ourselves, or fortify ourselves with material wealth and a quest to continually numb ourselves with alcohol, drugs, work, food, and other distractions. But contact with people living with

AIDS, immigrants, prisoners, abused women and children, the homeless, the outcasts, or anyone who is lonely will ignite the fire of the Holy Spirit. Courageous efforts to comfort are invariably graced with a miraculous spiritual healing.

To begin, it is important to be kind to each other. We respond to others when we feel respected, valued, and loved. So if we are kind to each person we meet, we will send a ripple that will touch others in many wonderful and unknown ways. In the end, all we can really do is little things, one at a time.

The Power of Simple Acts of Kindness

One day I received a call from the principal of St. Teresa's Grammar School in Runnemede, New Jersey. She asked if I could talk to the teachers on the subject of motivation. I sometimes give PTA talks to parents about motivating their children, so I said I would give it a try. There were about fifteen women, some religious, some in their sixties and seventies, some younger. I asked them to write a short paragraph about the teacher who influenced them the most. The first read what she had written to the group. She was a religious sister about fifty years of age. She told us that she had recently received a telephone call from a young man who said he was in her first grade class during the first year that she had taught. She didn't remember him at all. That year was just a blur to her. He made a date to visit with her. When they sat down, he told her that he was planning on getting married shortly. He had been in counseling because he had been abused by his father as a boy. His counselor had told him to visit with an adult who treated him kindly when he was a child. He asked the sister if she remembered Jimmy McFadden. She did not remember him either. He said that one day he got into a fight with Jimmy McFadden, and she broke it up. He thought he was in big trouble when she told him to report to the convent after school.

When he sat down, she brought him cookies and milk and just talked with him. She had forgotten all about it. He never will.

The second to speak up was an older sister who told us of a sister who was strict, caring, and a very good teacher. She was giving the standard account you would expect from another teacher. She also said in passing that this sister had visited her one Saturday morning after her father died. And she continued on with her standard account. I stopped her and repeated — "and she visited you one Saturday morning just after your father died." She then shed some tears and acknowledged that was how this teacher influenced her the most.

Then the teachers wrote of the students who they believed influenced them the most. One middle-aged woman talked of a seventh grade girl who pestered her. She said the girl's parents were going through a divorce and the child was really upset. So she listened to her often. Then she remembered that the teacher who influenced her the most was a woman who listened to her in seventh grade. She did not say what she had been going through. She too shed some tears when she remembered.

I listened as the teachers told of the power of simple acts of kindness. We were all in tears most of the time. Selfless acts of generosity are powerful forces. We can be kind and generous wherever we are, whatever our position. Afterward, I thought of how many times these teachers must have done kind, thoughtful, and loving things for children. We sow what we do not reap. We reap what others have sown. Some day I expect we will all be able to see how our kind acts have sent ripples of love throughout eternity.

Prayer

Jesus told us to pray and ask for what we want and it will be given. He knows that God has to respond to certain prayers. I don't think we can count on responses to prayers for good weather, a better job, or to cure an illness. I am as puzzled as the next person as to why we have such terrible things as earthquakes, hurricanes, tsunamis, and so on. But this I do know. If you ask God to see more clearly and to love God and everyone more dearly, your prayers will gradually be answered. God's will is to grant us the kingdom. I am sure that God desires us to know how much we are loved and for us to love each other. God has entrusted us with the custody of our children, our parents, and our friends and has given us gifts to share: to teach, to protect, to care for and rescue each other, especially the least among us, those in greatest need. One prayer I have prayed fervently for years is, "To see you more clearly, to love you more dearly, and to follow you more nearly." This is the kind of prayer that Jesus was talking about when he told us to ask. He knows that God has to respond to this kind of prayer. The Prayer of St. Francis of Assisi says it all.

> Lord, make me an instrument of your peace:
> Where there is hatred, let me sow love
> Where there is injury, pardon
> Where there is discord, unity
> Where there is doubt, faith
> Where there is error, truth
> Where there is despair, hope
> Where there is sadness, joy
> Where there is darkness, light.
> Oh Divine Master, grant that I may not so much seek:
> To be consoled, as to console
> To be understood, as to understand
> To be loved, as to love
> For it is in giving, that we receive
> It is in pardoning, that we are pardoned
> It is in dying, that we are born to eternal life.

St. Francis's prayers were answered and ours will be too. You have to believe. And if you don't, you can beg for the gift of greater faith. It really works. It will be given.

If we practice taking time every day to sit still, to empty ourselves and let the chatter of our minds pass, gradually we will find ourselves in touch with the Holy Spirit of God within us. I think centering prayer is a wonderful way to get in touch with God's Holy Spirit within. The goal is to sit still every day, perhaps twenty minutes in the morning or twenty minutes before dinner, or both, and empty ourselves of thoughts and plans, and to become still. When we notice our mind wander, as it surely will, we simply say a mantra such as, "Jesus," "Come," "Holy Spirit," "I'm yours," or a word or a phrase that helps you let go of your thoughts and remember you are in the presence of God. Gradually, in that space where we are empty and still we will feel the presence of God. Any time of the day, upon awakening, while walking, while driving, or before sleep we can repeat our mantra and invite God's Holy Spirit. Gradually through unceasing prayer we will find countless ways to become instruments of God's love. We will then experience the joy that results from our spiritual hunger being fed as we are in touch with those who suffer. Perhaps through grace and prayer we will come to recognize the Crucified Christ in our sisters and brothers who suffer tremendous injustice. Perhaps we will be able to recognize the Resurrected Christ within others and in ourselves. Eventually through grace, prayer, and persistence, we will find our beloved in everyone we encounter.

Epilogue

If Only You Knew

When I was hungry, I know you would have fed me if you knew where I was. But you didn't know me. How could you know me? You never held and fed a baby like me before. You never held a baby too hungry to cry.

When I was lonely, you didn't know where I was. I lived in a dangerous place. I know you are afraid to go where I live. It's not safe where I live.

When I was sick, you thought the doctors and hospitals wouldn't turn me away. How could you know?

When I was homeless, you gave me some money, and I felt your prayers. But you couldn't have known the terror in that shelter and why I stayed on the street. You didn't know that I was sick — that I saw demons but they were real. How could you know? We never talked.

When I lost my little girl because we had no money for medicine, you didn't know what I needed. You didn't know where we were. We lived so far from you. They call it the Third World.

When I sent my boy to sell lottery tickets, you didn't know us. You didn't know I wanted him to go to school but I needed his earnings for food. We were so far away from you. We spoke in a foreign tongue. How could you know us?

A Haitian boy.

You didn't know why my boy didn't come home that night. We knew. His father took his money and bought alcohol and beat him so many times. He stayed in the streets and never came back to me. How could you have known he didn't come home?

You didn't know how the kids live on the street — and what the older ones and the men do to the little ones. And you didn't know about the drugs. How could you? You didn't know that I am with those boys too, and they do it to me. But how could you know?

When I pleaded for fair wages, they tortured me. We made your clothes. But you didn't know who we were. You didn't know what they did to those of us who spoke for fair wages and safe conditions. How could you know how far they'd go?

When I gathered your food and got sick from the chemicals, you couldn't know. You didn't know what the chemicals did to our children. You didn't know of the nightmares they caused. How could you know? You never gathered foods from the fields. You never touched or smelled the chemicals.

Did you know that my children work in the garbage? They collect paper and bottles and cans. And they sell them so we can eat. It's so dangerous there. Surely you don't know of the dangers — of the gas explosions and fires, of the chemicals and disease. But what can I do? I have no other way to feed my children. But you didn't know.

When we spoke for our land, our ancestors' land, they slaughtered us. They mutilated and tortured me so many times in so many ways. They smashed my children against the rocks. They raped and killed my wife and daughters. They did it for the land owners who sell you your food. They did it to me. But how could you know what they did? It wasn't on the news. None of your friends could tell you. We live so far from you.

You were so busy. You had your children. You rocked them and sang to them and helped them with their homework and read them stories and tucked them in and taught them to pray. You took them to soccer practice and baseball games, to dance classes and music lessons. You were so busy.

You worshiped me often. You met with your friends and talked of your love for me. I heard your love songs. And I heard your praise and thanks. You thought I was in heaven. That's what they told you. You just didn't know.

You worked so hard. I know it wasn't easy. They'd fire you so quickly. So you had to work hard to provide for your family. I know you were afraid.

But you shouldn't have feared. I sent you food from the fields so you wouldn't go hungry. I sent you your clothes, and I sent you my love. Even when you didn't know it or believe it, I loved you always.

When you smashed my baby against the rocks, you didn't know it was me. You were so afraid of the sergeant. You didn't know what to do. You didn't want to kill me. He said he'd kill you if you didn't do it. You were so afraid.

When you took my money for alcohol and beat me, you didn't know that I'd go to the streets and never come home. You didn't know what they'd do to me. I know you loved me. You just didn't know how much I loved you.

And when I needed money for my daughter's medicine, I know you would have bought it for her, if only you knew where we were.

I loved you when I was hungry and you had extra food. I know you would have fed me if you could — if you saw me, if you held me. I'm sure you wouldn't have left me to starve, if you knew who I was.

If only you knew. I come to you through the children. I come a million times a day. But look what is done to me. I'm hungry and sick, beaten and abandoned. I'm tortured and mutilated, abused and battered.

I'm waiting in the children. Can you hear me? Listen. I'm in your heart — your Sacred Heart. And you are always in my heart.

Come to me. Come to the children. Don't be afraid. I'll mend your heart.

Can you hear me? I love you. I love you. I love you. If only you knew.

— VG

Notes

Introduction

1. Bread for the World Institute's Offering of Letters, "Hunger and Health Facts" (Silver Spring, MD, 2004), 1.
2. Ibid., 13.
3. Paul Farmer, *Pathologies of Power* (Berkeley: University of California Press, 2003), 23.
4. Donald H. Dunson, *No Room at the Table: Earth's Most Vulnerable Children* (Maryknoll, NY: Orbis, 2003), 25.

1 / Awakening to the Hidden Violence

1. Chris Schweitzer, "Information in the Land of Oz," *Catholic Peace Voice*, Pax Christi USA (Winter–Spring 2001): 10.
2. Ibid., 11.
3. Ronald Sider, *Rich Christians in an Age of Hunger: Moving from Affluence to Generosity* (Dallas: Word Publishing, 1997), 50.
4. The amount of money privately donated by people in the United States in 2004 was twenty times larger than official U.S. overseas aid, but only 2.1 percent of donations were designated "international" according to the World Development Report 2005, *www.aafrc.org*.

2 / Neocolonialism — The Search for the Most Desperate Workers

1. National Labor Committee, *No More Sweatshops* (New York, 2000).
2. Garrett Brown, "Vulnerable Workers in the Global Economy," *Occupational Hazards* (April 2004): 29.
3. National Labor Committee, *No More Sweatshops*.
4. National Labor Committee, *It Does Not Have to Be Like This* (New York, 2005).

3 / International Financial Institutions — Instruments of
Development or Violence?

1. Michel Chossudovsky, *Globalization of Poverty in the New World Order,* 2nd ed. (Oro, Ontario: Global Outlook, 2003), 48.
2. Duncan Green, *Silent Revolution: The Rise and Crisis of Market Economics in Latin America* (New York: Monthly Review Press, 2003), 153.
3. The World Bank Group and National Geographic Maps, "A Global Agenda to End Poverty" (Washington, DC, 2005).
4. Ibid., 165.
5. Ibid.
6. Ibid., 109.
7. Jeff Faux, *The Global Class War* (Hoboken, NJ: John Wiley and Sons, 2006), 160.
8. Ibid.

4 / How the Poor Suffer

1. Christina Alexander, "A Way of Giving," *Company* (a magazine of the American Jesuits) (Summer 1996): 12.
2. Ibid., 13.
3. Miki Takahashi and Carolyn Cederlof, *Street Children in Central America: An Overview,* Human Development Department, World Bank Group, April 21, 2000, 1–3.
4. "Stolen Childhood: Girl and Boy Victims of Sexual Exploitation in Mexico," as reported in *Profiting from Abuse* (New York: UNICEF, 2001), 5.
5. "Brazil: Children Suffer Abuses," *LatinAmerica Press,* October 18, 1990, 7.
6. Kevin Bales, *Disposable People* (Berkeley: University of California Press, 1999), 4.
7. Phyllis Kilbourn and Marjorie McDermid, *Sexually Exploited Children: Working to Protect and Heal* (Monrovia, CA: MARC, 1998), 9.
8. Ibid., 10.
9. Christopher P. Baker, "Prostitution: Child Chattel Lure Tourists for Sex," *National Times,* August–September 1995, 8, as reported in Kilbourn and McDermid, *Sexually Exploited Children,* 11.
10. Patricia Green, "Impact of Sexual Exploitation on Children," in Kilbourn and McDermid, *Sexually Exploited Children,* 54.
11. Ibid., 55.

12. United Nations Children's Fund Report, "Poverty and Children, Lessons for the 1990s for Least Developed Countries" (New York: UNICEF, 2001), 22–23.

13. Maryknoll Office of Global Concerns, *News Notes* (September–October 2005): 22.

14. Maryknoll Office of Global Concerns, *News Notes* (November–December 2005): 24.

15. Ibid., 25.

16. United Nations Children's Fund, *Poverty Reduction Begins With Children* (New York: UNICEF, 2000), 1.

5 / Do the World Bank and IMF Help or Hinder?

1. Kevin Clarke, "Someone's Got to Give," *U.S. Catholic* (December 2004): 29.

2. Joseph E. Stiglitz, *Globalization and Its Discontents* (New York: W. W. Norton, 2003), xiv.

3. Ibid., 15.

4. Ibid., 259.

5. Chossudovsky, *Globalization of Poverty and the New World Order*, 35.

6. Jean-Bertrand Aristide, cited in Haiti Action Committee, *Hidden from the Headlines: The U.S. War against Haiti* (Berkeley, 2004).

7. Chossudovsky, *Globalization of Poverty and the New World Order*, 61.

8. Ibid., 60, quoted from Mohsin Khan, "The Macroeconomics Effect of Fund Supported Adjustment Programs," *IMF Staff Papers* 30, no. 2 (1999): 196, 222.

9. GeorgeAnne Potter, *Deeper Than Debt: Economic Globalization and the Poor* (London: Latin American Bureau, 2000), 27.

10. United Nations, *The Inequality Predicament: Report on the World Social Situation 2005* (New York, 2005), 27.

11. Ibid., 1.

12. James Galbraith quoted in Farmer, *Pathologies of Power*, 303.

13. Public Citizen Product ID 9013, *Another America Is Possible: The Impact of NAFTA on the U.S. Latino Community and Lessons for Future Trade Agreements* (Washington, DC, 2004), 5.

14. Ibid., 4–8.

15. Chossudovsky, *Globalization of Poverty and the New World Order*, 31.

16. Ibid.

17. Ibid., 33.
18. Ibid.

6 / Keeping Unfair Structures in Place

1. James Hodge and Linda Cooper, Disturbing the Peace (Maryknoll, NY: Orbis, 2004), 170.
2. Chossudovsky, Globalization of Poverty and the New World Order, 19–20.
3. Green, Silent Revolution, 33.
4. James Hodge and Linda Cooper, "Roots of Abu Ghraib in CIA Techniques: Fifty Years of Refining, Teaching Torture Found in Interrogation Manuals," National Catholic Reporter, November 5, 2004, 12.
5. Ibid., 11.
6. Hodge and Cooper, Disturbing the Peace, 166.

7 / The Uses of Slaves in the Global Economy

1. Bales, Disposable People, 8.
2. Helene O'Sullivan, M.M., "Stopping Traffic," Maryknoll (November 2003): 30.
3. Bales, Disposable People, 18.
4. David Binder, "Southeastern Europe Nations Unite to Battle Sex Trafficking," New York Times International, August 15, 2004, 13.
5. Gloria Macapagal Arroua, "Getting Our Act Together," in United Nations Children's Fund, Profiting from Abuse: An Investigation into Sexual Exploitation of Children (New York: UNICEF, 2001), 4.
6. Ibid., 7.
7. Ibid.
8. Pamela Shifman and Ken Franzblau, "Trafficking: Legislative Responses," in United Nations Children's Fund, Profiting from Abuse, 12–13.
9. Kevin Hall, "Hidden Away, Slaves Still Toil in Brazil," Philadelphia Inquirer (September 7, 2004): 1.
10. Ibid., 59.

8 / The Politics of Food

1. United Nations Development Program, Manifesto Against Hunger and Underdevelopment (UNDP Staff Publication, vol. 9, no. 4, 1981), 1.
2. Bread for the World Institute 2006 Offering of Letters, "Hunger and Poverty Facts," 12.

3. Poster of the Institute for Food and Development Policy, designed by Kathy McGilvery, "Hunger Myths and Facts" (San Francisco, October 1998).

4. Jean-Bertrand Aristide, *Eyes of the Heart: Seeking a Path for the Poor in the Age of Globalization* (Monroe, ME: Common Courage Press, 2000), 11.

5. Cesar Ferrari and Carlos Novoa, S.J., "An Imbalance of Power: How U.S. Agricultural Subsidies Undermine Free Trade," *America* (March 1, 2004): 20.

6. Steve Chapman, "Handouts Don't Solve Africa's Problems," *Philadelphia Inquirer* (July 17, 2003): 19.

7. Editorial, *Business Week* (August 6, 2004): 108.

8. Sider, *Rich Christians in an Age of Hunger,* 166.

9 / Women and Children Are Hurt the Most

1. Sider, *Rich Christians in an Age of Hunger,* 177.

2. Ibid.

3. Ibid.

4. Ibid.

5. Ibid., 53.

6. Ibid.

7. Robin Broad, "General Principle and Gender, Hemispheric Social Alliance," *Global Backlash: Citizen Initiatives for a Just World Economy* (New York: Rowman and Littlefield, 2002), 52.

8. Ibid., 53.

9. United Nations Development Program, International Poverty Centre, *In Focus* (New York City, March 2004), 13.

10. Millennium Project, "Fast Facts: The Faces of Poverty" (New York, 2005), 1.

11. United Nations Development Program, International Poverty Centre, "Measuring Child Poverty and Deprivation," *In Focus* (New York, March 2004), 1.

12. Bread for the World Institute, "World Hunger and Poverty: How They Fit Together" (Washington DC, 2003), 2.

13. Ibid., 1.

14. UNICEF/UNAIDS, 2003, "UNICEF, UNAIDS Applaud Milestone in Coordinated Global Response to Children Orphaned Due to AIDS," joint press release, Geneva: October 21, 2005, as reported in *Facts and Figures on HIV/AIDS,* United Nations Development Fund for Women, *www.unifem.org/gender_issues/HIV_AIDS/facts_figures.php.*

15. Kevin Clarke, "Innocence Lost," *U.S. Catholic* (March 2006): 36.

16. Nicholas D. Kristof, "Slavery in Our Time," *New York Times,* January 22, 2006, 17.

17. Chossudovsky, *Globalization of Poverty and the New World Order,* 66.

18. Mithre J. Sandrasagra, *Globalization Heightening Gender Inequalities* (New York: Third World Network, 2000), 3.

19. Ann Whitehead, *Failing Women, Sustaining Poverty: Gender Poverty and Reduction Strategy Papers,* report for the UK Gender and Development Network (London: Gender and Development Network and Christian Aid, May 2003), 14.

20. United Nations Development Fund for Women, *Violence against Women: Facts and Figures* (New York, 2005), 1.

21. Ibid., 2.

22. Ibid.

23. Ibid., 3.

24. Ibid.

25. United Nations Population Foundation/Engender Health Report, *Obstetric Fistula Needs Assessment Report: Findings from Nine African Countries* (New York, 2000), 4.

26. The American Friends Foundation for Childbirth Injuries makes it easy to donate $450 to the Fistula Hospital to restore a woman's health and dignity (*www.fistulahospital.org*). For more information on obstetric fistula see *www.wfmic.org, www.unfpa.org.*

27. Bread for the World Institute's Offering of Letters, "Hunger and Health Facts," 13.

28. United Nations Development Fund for Women, *Facts and Figures on HIV/AIDS* (New York, 2005), 1.

29. Ibid., 2.

30. The UN Commission for Latin America and the Caribbean, "Gender and HIV/AIDS," *Gender Dialogues* (October 14, 2005): 1.

31. United Nations Development Fund for Women, *Facts and Figures on HIV/AIDS,* 1.

32. Françoise Heritier, "De la violence," as quoted in Farmer, *Pathologies of Power,* 7.

33. Farmer, *Pathologies of Power,* 173.

10 / Violence against Latino Workers in El Salvador and the United States

1. Abel Valenzuela Jr., Nik Theodra, Edwin Melendez, Anna Cruz Gonzalez, "On the Corner: Day Labor in the United States," Center for

Urban Economic Development, University of Illinois at Chicago (January 2006), *www.uic.edu/cuppa/uicued/Publications/recent/onthecorner.pdf*.

2. Justin Prichard and Julie Reed, "A Mexican Worker Dies Each Day, AP Finds," *Safer Times* (Philadelphia), no. 103 (Spring 2004).

3. Ibid., 4.

4. Valenzuela et al., "On the Corner," 13.

5. Personal experience of author.

11 / The Need for a Theology That Liberates

1. Gustavo Gutiérrez, *A Theology of Liberation* (Maryknoll, NY: Orbis, 1973), 13.

2. Dom Helder Camara, *Revolution through Peace,* ed. Ruth Nanda Anshen, trans. Amparo McLean (New York: Harper and Row, 1971).

3. Jon Sobrino, *Witnesses to the Kingdom* (Maryknoll, NY: Orbis, 2003), 80.

4. Ibid., 158.

5. Ibid., 40.

6. Conversation by the author with Father Ed Moore, Maryknoll priest who served in Guatemala during the civil war.

12 / Awakening to the Reality of Suffering

1. Green, *Silent Revolution,* 63.

2. Conversation of author with Marie Dennis.

3. Barbara Fraser and Paul Jeffrey, "Looking Ahead: Church Groups Seek New Models of Solidarity," *National Catholic Reporter* (November 26, 2004): 15.

4. "Let's Put the Eucharist to Work," *U.S. Catholic* (July 2005): 15.

5. To start a "Catholic School Uniform Program," contact Elisa Meredith, New York State Labor-Religion Coalition at *elisam@labor-religion.org* or Handcrafting Justice (*www.giveworld.org*).

Bibliography

Bales, Kevin. *Disposable People: New Slavery in the Global Economy.* Berkeley: University of California Press, 1999.

Broad, Robin. *Global Backlash: Citizen Initiatives for a Just World Economy.* New York: Rowman and Littlefield, 2002.

Byron, William, ed. *The Causes of World Hunger.* Ramsey, NJ: Paulist Press, 1982.

Chomsky, Noam. *Profit over People: Neoliberalism and Global Order.* New York: Seven Stories Press, 1999.

Chossudovsky, Michel. *The Globalization of Poverty and the New World Order.* 2nd ed. Oro, Ontario: Global Outlook, 2003.

DeBerri, Edward P., Peter J. Henriot, James Hug, and Michael J. Schultheis. *Catholic Social Teaching: Our Best Kept Secret.* 4th rev. ed. Maryknoll, NY: Orbis, 2003.

Dunson, Donald. *No Room at the Table: Earth's Most Vulnerable Children.* Maryknoll, NY: Orbis, 2003.

Farmer, Paul. *Pathologies of Power: Health, Human Rights, and the New War on the Poor.* Berkeley: University of California Press, 2003.

———. *The Uses of Haiti.* Monroe, ME: Common Courage Press, 2003.

George, Susan. *The Debt Boomerang: How Third World Debt Harms Us All.* San Francisco: Westview Press, 1992.

Green, Duncan. *Silent Revolution: The Rise and Crisis of Market Economics in Latin America.* New York: Monthly Review Press, 2003.

Gutiérrez, Gustavo. *A Theology of Liberation: History, Politics, and Salvation.* Maryknoll, NY: Orbis, 1973.

Harbury, Jennifer. *Truth, Torture, and the American Way: The History and Consequences of U.S. Involvement in Torture* . Boston: Beacon, 2005.

Hodge, James, and Linda Cooper. *Disturbing the Peace: The Story of Father Roy Bourgeois and the Movement to Close the School of the Americas.* Maryknoll, NY: Orbis, 2004.

Johnson, George S. *Beyond Guilt and Powerlessness.* Minneapolis: Augsburg Fortress, 1989.

Kilbourn, Phyllis, and Majorie McDermid. *Sexually Exploited Children: Working to Protect and Heal.* Monrovia, CA: MARC Publishing, 1998.

Kwitny, Jonathan. *Endless Enemies: The Making of an Unfriendly World.* New York: Congdon and Weed, 1984.

Perry, John, *Torture: Religious Ethics and National Security.* Maryknoll, NY: Orbis, 2005.

Potter, George Anne. *Deeper Than Debt: Economic Globalization and the Poor.* London: Latin American Bureau, 2000.

Sider, Ronald J. *Rich Christians in an Age of Hunger: Moving from Affluence to Generosity.* Dallas: Word Publishing, 1997.

Sobrino, Jon. *Witnesses to the Kingdom: The Martyrs of El Salvador and the Crucified Peoples.* Maryknoll, NY: Orbis, 2003.

Stiglitz, Joseph E. *Globalization and Its Discontents.* New York: W. W. Norton, 2003.

Wise, Timothy A., Hilda Salazar, and Laura Carlsen, eds. *Confronting Globalization: Economic Integration and Popular Resistance in Mexico.* Bloomfield, CT: Kumarian Press, 2003.

Index

Numbers in *italics* indicate photographs or figures.